Prehistoric Origami

Dinosaurs and Other Creatures

Other books by John Montroll:

Origami Sculptures

Origami Sea Life by John Montroll and Robert Lang

Origami Inside-Out

African Animals in Origami

Animal Origami for the Enthusiast

Origami for the Enthusiast

Easy Origami

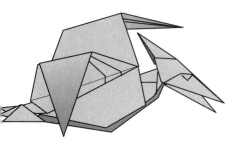

PREHISTORIC ORIGAMI

Dinosaurs and Other Creatures

John Montroll

Dover Publications, Inc.

New York

To Carol Ann, Kathleen, Martha, Mark, Jan, and Mark

Published in Canada by General Publishing Company, Ltd., 30 Lesmill Road, Don Mills, Toronto, Ontario.
Published in the United Kingdom by Constable and Company, Ltd., 3 The Lanchesters, 162–164 Fulham Palace Road, London W6 9ER.

This Dover edition, first published in 1990, is an unabridged and unaltered republication of the work originally published in 1989 by Antroll Publishing Company, Maryland.

Manufactured in the United States of America
Dover Publications, Inc., 31 East 2nd Street, Mineola, N.Y. 11501

Library of Congress Cataloging-in-Publication Data

Montroll, John.
    Prehistoric origami : dinosaurs and other creatures / John Montroll.
        p.   cm.
    Originally published: Maryland: Antroll Pub. Co., c1989
    ISBN 0-486-26588-9 (pbk.)
    1. Origami.   2. Dinosaurs in art.   I. Title.
TT870.M573   1990
736'.982—dc20
                                                  90-13960
                                                    CIP

Introduction

My goal with this collection of original projects has been to use origami to create an accurate and aesthetically pleasing collection of prehistoric animals. The presentation of animals in this book reflects the most current paleontological theories, from nomenclature (the Apatosaurus has replaced the recently decanonized Brontosaurus from my paper menagerie) to fine structural detail (note the dorsal plating on the Stegosaurus). I hope that the resulting work provides the reader/user with both a technically accurate survey of these extinct creatures and many hours of artistic pleasure.

Although any square paper can be used for the projects in this book, the best material is origami paper. Origami paper is sold in many hobby shops, and can be purchased by mail from The Friends of the Origami Center of America, 15 West 77 Street, New York, NY 10024-5192. Large sheets of paper are easier to work with than smaller ones. Origami paper is colored on one side and white on the other. In my diagrams, the shading represents the colored side of the paper.

Origami paper, and a catalog of other available craft books, can also be ordered from Dover Publications, Inc., 31 East 2nd St., Mineola, NY 11501.

This book is a combination of the old and modern. The ancient art here is illustrated step-by-step with graphics produced on a computer. The illustrations conform to the internationally accepted Randlett-Yoshizawa conventions. The directions for each project have been submitted to experienced origami artists, and I thank the many friends whose suggestions have helped me improve the clarity of my illustrations and explanations.

Other friends have helped in other ways. Martha Landy has provided an excellent introduction and background notes on the animals. Ms. Landy teaches students with special needs in New Brunswick, New Jersey. Her class has produced "Dinosaur Day" for the past eight years at John Adams Elementary School. Her students research and explain dinosaurs and celebrate them with the entire school. In addition to her personal passion for dinosaurs, Ms. Landy finds them one of the most motivating educational tools.

Rosalind Joyce has made valuable contributions to this book through her research and suggestions on the techniques of wet folding. Her methods enable origami artists to infuse their work with more three-dimensional detail than most of us had thought possible. Don Shall helped with computer graphics. My brother Andy helped throughout this project. I give thanks to these talented people, without whose help this book could not have been completed.

John Montroll

Contents

Mountain & Volcano
*
Page 12

Cracked Dinosaur Egg
*
Page 14

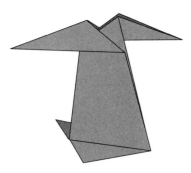

Prehistoric Tree
*
Page 16

Parasaurolophus
**
Page 20

Struthiomimus
**
Page 25

Kuehneosaurus
**
Page 29

Archaeoptryx
**
Page 33

Pterodactylus
**
Page 38

Quetzalcoatlus
**
Page 43

Rhamphorynchus
**
Page 49

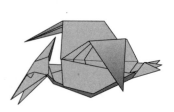

Pteranodon
***
Page 54

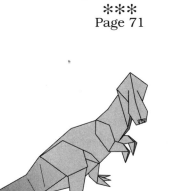

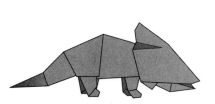
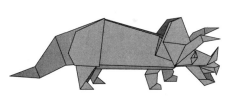
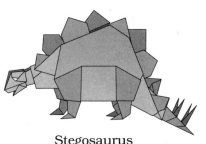

Contents 7

To Define a Dinosaur

Dinosaurs lived in the Mesozoic (mezz-oh-ZOE-ik) Era which began 225 million years ago and lasted for 155 million years. Mesozoic means "middle life". The era is divided into three periods.

Dinosaurs appeared on earth during the Triassic (try-ASS-ik) Period. It lasted for 45 million years. All the continents were connected in one giant land mass. There were only a few kinds of dinosaur. These were mostly small, quick, meat eaters.

The Jurassic (joo-RASS-ik) Period began 180 million years ago and lasted for 45 million years. The continents began to move apart and shallow seas and swamps formed. The climate was tropical. The largest dinosaurs lived at this time.

The Cretaceous (kre-TAY-shus) Period is the time the most varieties of dinosaurs lived. It was 65 million years long. The continents were well separated. The climate was seasonal and flowers appeared on earth for the first time.

To be a dinosaur an animal must have a specific skull and hip structure. One way scientists classify reptiles is by the number of holes in the back of the skull. These holes may be to accommodate jaw muscles. They lighten the weight of the skull. All dinosaurs are diapsids (di-AP-sids), having two holes in their skulls.

The Ornithischian (orn-ith-ISK-ee-an) dinosaurs have the two lower bones of the hip pointing towards the back. They have a beak-like addition to the jaw bone. Some were plant eaters and some were meat eaters. Ornithischian mean "bird-hipped". The Saurischian (sawr-ISK-ee-an) dinosaurs have each hip bone pointing in a different direction. They have a solid jaw and are meat eaters. Saurischian means "lizard-hipped".

All true dinosaurs were land dwellers. However, some dinosaurs, like many other land dwelling animals, would sometimes wade or swim.

Martha Landy

The Tyrannosaurus is an Ornithischian dinosaur which lived during the Cretaceous Period.

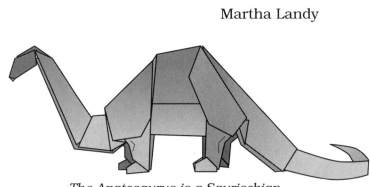

The Apatosaurus is a Saurischian dinosaur which lived during the Jurassic Period.

Wet Folding

Sometimes, you find that thick, textured, or leathery papers in your collection look like they would make wonderful origami, until you work with them. After very few folds, they become torn and ugly. If a favorite sheet has become old and brittle, it does not fold well, either; it breaks!

Before you give up on uncooperative paper, try wet folding. The results are greater flexibility and solid, long-lasting models. As the paper dries, its own adhesives hold your folds stiffly and permanently. (Purists ignore this: A drop or two of white GLUE to a cup of water adds body to soft paper.)

How much water should be used? The amount varies with the kind of paper you choose. Start by dampening the underside of your paper with a squeezed out washcloth or sponge. A spray bottle or wet hands work just as well. Soaking the paper makes it fall apart. If it gets too wet, wait until some water evaporates. Wet folding can be messy. Some papers flop apart when you least appreciate it.

Fold your models slowly and carefully, with fingertips, not nails. Sharp creases can tear. While you fold, notice how moisture evaporates from different papers at different rates. Re-wet parts of the model as you work, so that your paper stays flexible.

An added attraction is to make the model three dimensional. While it is still wet, the head, tail, legs, and body can be rolled or pinched to look like hollow, 3-D tubes. Many models will dry as you handle them and mold them into place. If others do not stay in position while you shape them, use paper clips or thin wire to keep them where you want them. The wire can pose each part, like a sculpture, creating the exact personality you prefer for the model. Remove wire and clips after the paper is dry.

Unlike foil that remembers every mistake you made, you can re-wet and re-fold small parts of your model without ruining it. This is helpful when making adjustments for free standing subjects.

Depending on the type of paper, your model will dry within a few minutes to overnight. If you discover that your masterpiece was made from waterproof, vinyl coated paper, just be more patient! From simple folds to the ridiculously complex, wet folding adds another dimension to your origami.

Rosalind Joyce

Symbols

Lines

— — — — — — — — — — Valley fold, fold in front.

—·—·—·—·—·—·—·—·— — Mountain fold, fold behind.

———————————— Crease line.

····························· X-ray or guide line.

Arrows

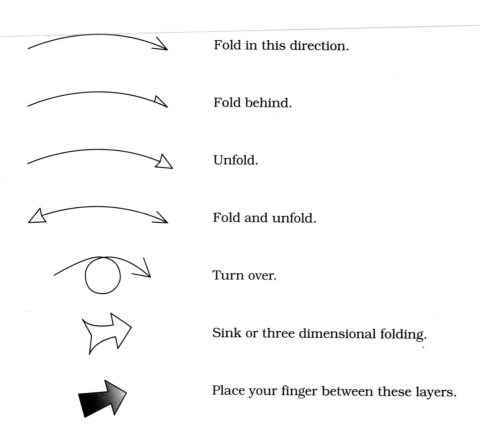

Fold in this direction.

Fold behind.

Unfold.

Fold and unfold.

Turn over.

Sink or three dimensional folding.

Place your finger between these layers.

Mountain and Volcano

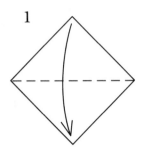

1

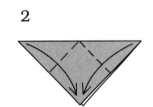

2

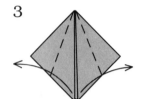

3

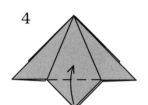

4

Fold both layers
up together.

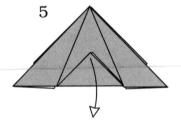

5

Unfold both layers.

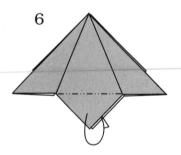

6

Fold the top layer inside.

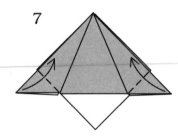

7

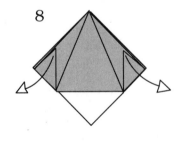

8

Unfold.

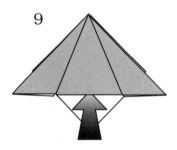

9

Place your finger inside. In
step 11, some paper will be
tucked inside this pocket. (You
can take your finger out.)

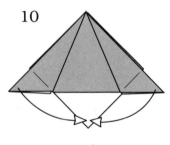

10

Unfold.

11

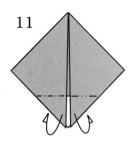

Tuck inside the pocket.

12

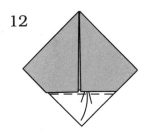

Tuck inside the pocket.

13

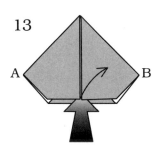

Place your finger inside to open and flatten the model so that A and B meet.

14

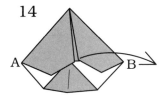

An intermediate step.

15

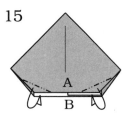

Fold the corners inside, repeat behind.

16

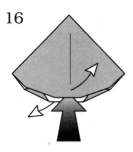

Open.

17

Mountain

18

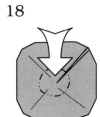

This is the top view of the mountain. To fold a volcano, push the top inside. This is a sink fold.

19

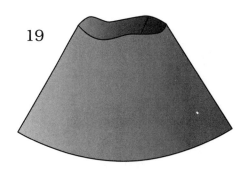

Volcano

Cracked Dinosaur Egg

1
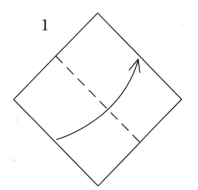

2
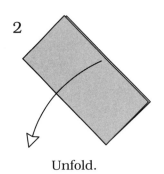

Unfold.

3
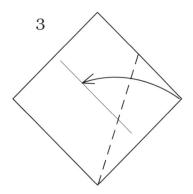

Fold the corner
to the center line.

4
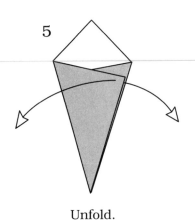

5
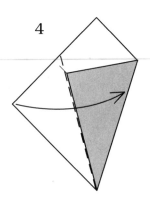

Unfold.

6
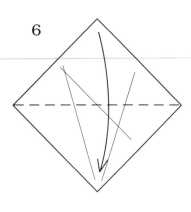

7

A   B

Fold the top layer to
the dotted lines so it
meets A and B.

8

Place your finger between
these layers. Let's call this
the prehistoric pocket. In
step 11 some paper will be
folded into it.

9

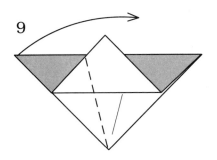

Fold along the crease.

10

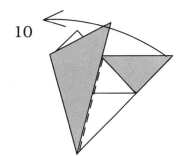

11

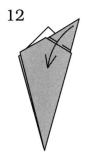

Tuck inside the prehistoric pocket.

12

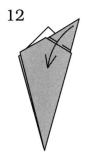

13

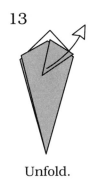

Unfold.

14

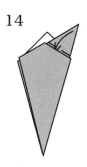

Tuck inside.

15

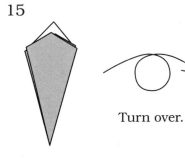

Turn over.

16

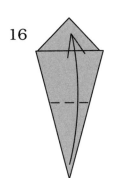

17

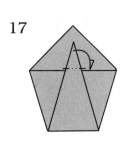

Tuck inside.

18

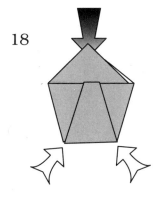

Place your finger all the way inside and squeeze on the two lower corners. Make the egg round and three-dimensional.

19

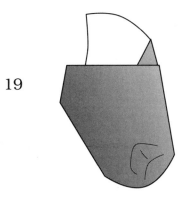

Cracked Dinosaur Egg

Prehistoric Tree

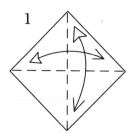

1

Fold and unfold.

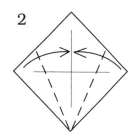

2

Kite-fold.

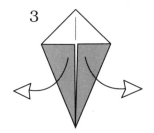

3

Unfold.

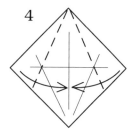

4

Kite-fold.

5

Squash-fold.

6

Squash-fold.

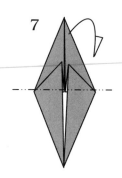

7

Fold behind.

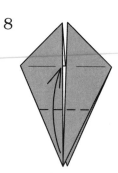

8

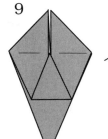

9

Turn over.

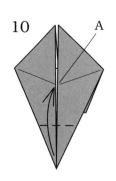

10

A

Fold to A.

11

Turn over.

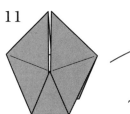

12

Rotate.

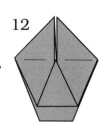

13
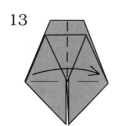

14
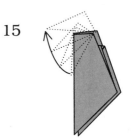
Slide up.

15
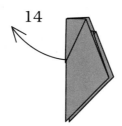
An intermediate step.

16
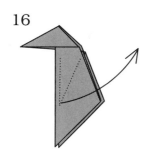
Slide the inside paper up.

17
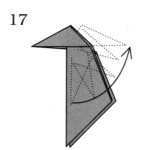
An intermediate step.

18
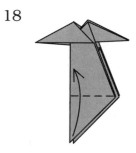
Fold the root up.

19
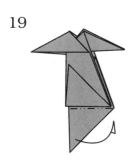
Fold behind. Fold the
roots half way down so
the tree can stand.

20
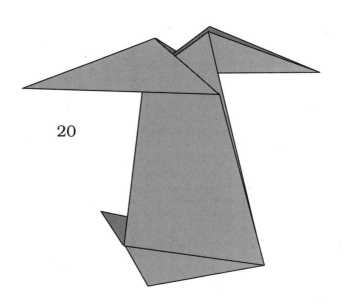

Prehistoric Tree

Bird Base

1

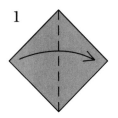

Fold in half.

2

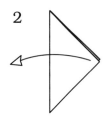

Unfold.

3

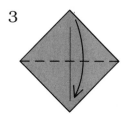

Fold in half.

4

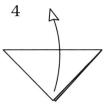

Unfold.

5

Turn over.

6

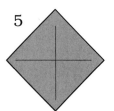

Book-fold.

7

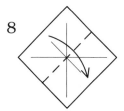

Unfold.

8

Book-fold.

9

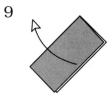

Unfold.

10

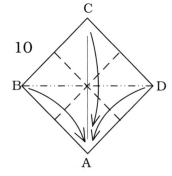

Collapse along the creases
so that corners B, C, and
D lie on top of A.

11

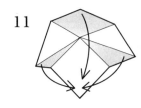

This is a three-dimensional
intermediate step.

12

This is the
Preliminary Fold.

13

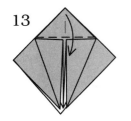

14

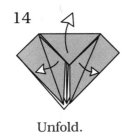

Unfold.

15

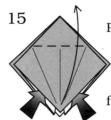

Place your fingers under the top layer as shown by the dark arrows. Fold the corner at the bottom to the top. Step 18 shows the finished fold.

16

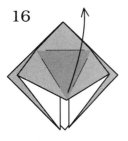

A three-dimensional intermediate step.

17

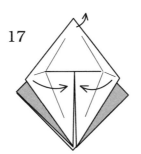

A three-dimensional intermediate step.

18

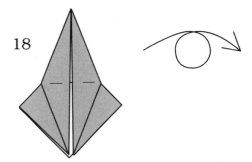

19

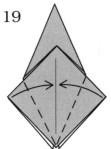

20

21

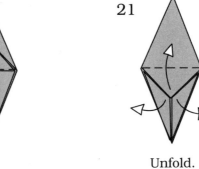

Unfold.

22

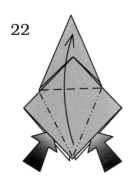

Fold the corner up (repeat steps 15–18).

23

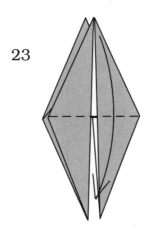

Repeat behind.

24

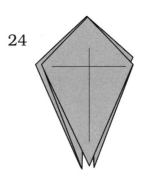

Bird Base

Parasaurolophus

par-a-SAUR-oh-loaf-us

A swamp dwelling, Cretaceous plant eater, this dinosaur was 33 feet long. The webbed feet and bill were not the only similarities to ducks. The long tubular crest on the top of the head may have enabled it to honk like a goose. It had grinding teeth in the back of the mouth. Parasaurolophus means "almost crest head" and it may have been the female to Corythosaurus.

Begin with the Bird Base (page 18).

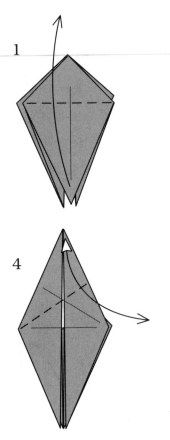

1

2

3

Unfold.

4

Fold and unfold.

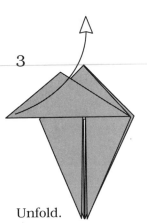

5

A rabbit ear will now be formed. To begin, fold the two sides of the tip towards the center. Step 7 shows the completed rabbit ear.

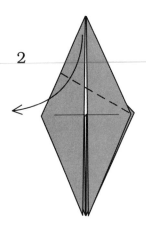

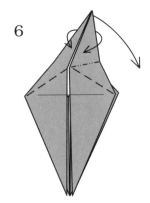

6

This three-dimensional figure shows the rabbit ear in progress.

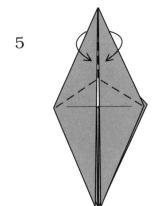

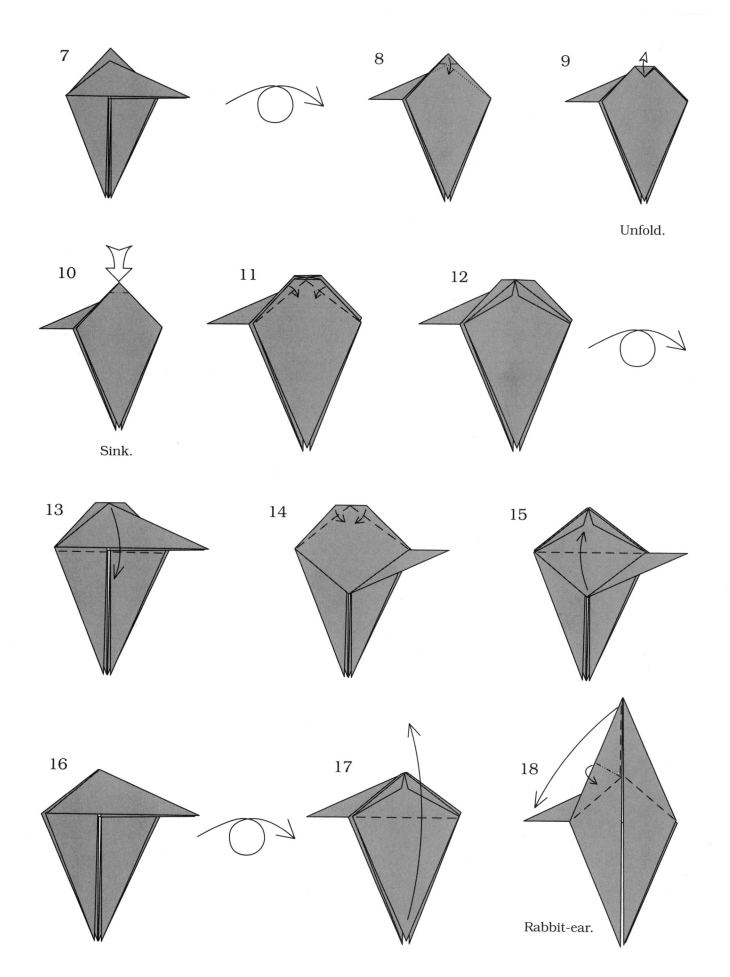

7

8

9

Unfold.

10

Sink.

11

12

13

14

15

16

17

18

Rabbit-ear.

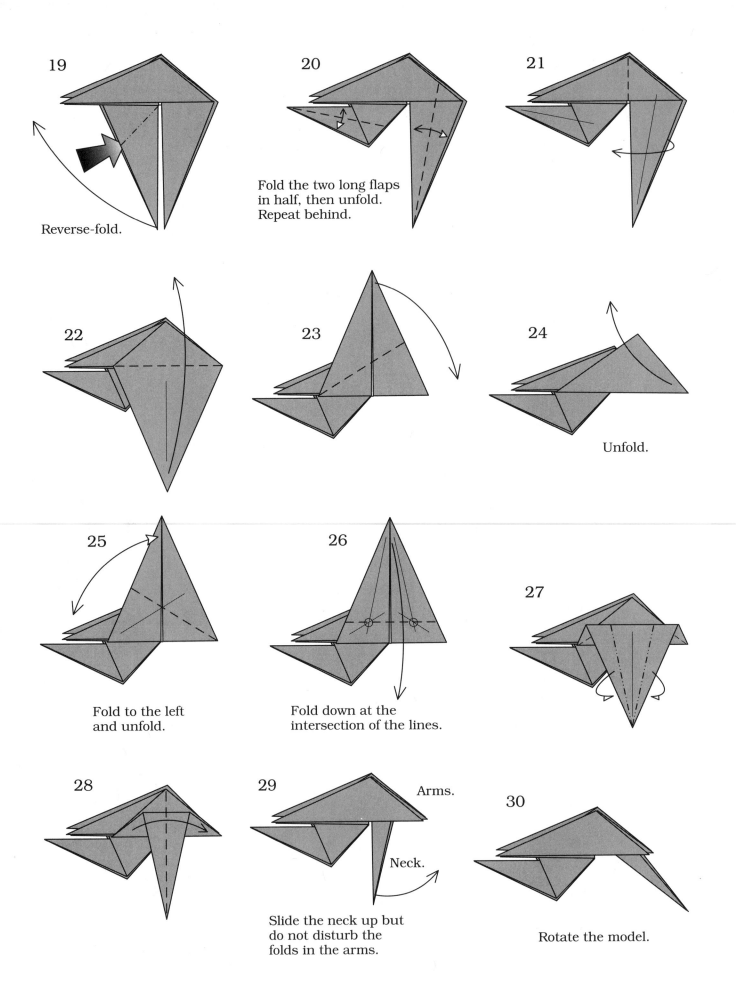

19

Reverse-fold.

20

Fold the two long flaps
in half, then unfold.
Repeat behind.

21

22

23

24

Unfold.

25

Fold to the left
and unfold.

26

Fold down at the
intersection of the lines.

27

28

29

Arms.

Neck.

Slide the neck up but
do not disturb the
folds in the arms.

30

Rotate the model.

31

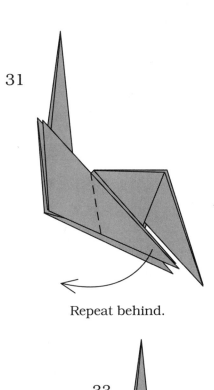

Repeat behind.

32

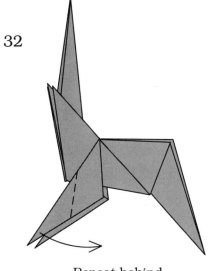

Repeat behind.

33

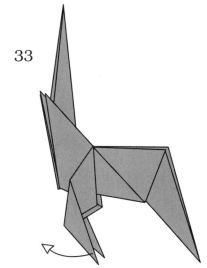

Unfold, repeat behind.

34

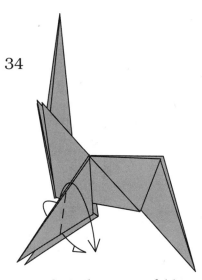

Outside-reverse-fold,
repeat behind.

35

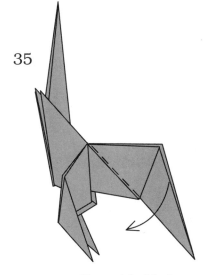

Repeat behind.

36

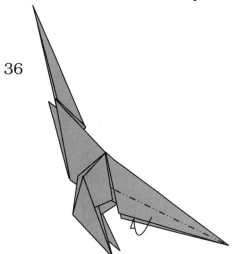

Tuck this paper inside the
most central layer near the
top of the tail. Repeat behind.

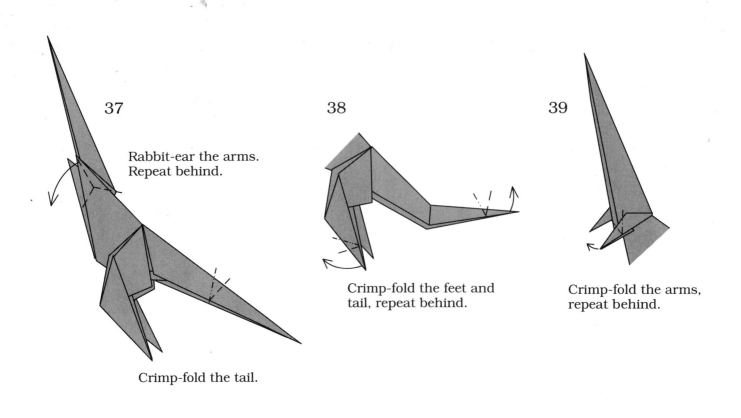

37 Rabbit-ear the arms.
Repeat behind.

Crimp-fold the tail.

38

Crimp-fold the feet and
tail, repeat behind.

39

Crimp-fold the arms,
repeat behind.

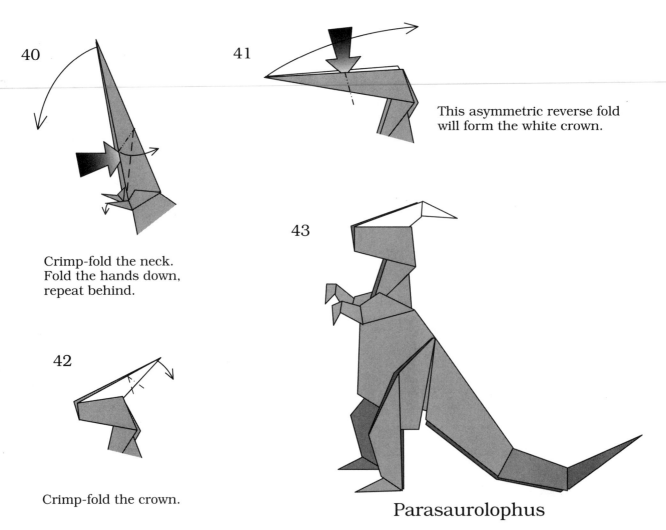

40

Crimp-fold the neck.
Fold the hands down,
repeat behind.

41

This asymmetric reverse fold
will form the white crown.

42

Crimp-fold the crown.

43

Parasaurolophus

Struthiomimus

strooth-ee-oh-MIM-us

This 12 foot long Cretaceous dinosaur was probably as swift as an ostrich. The name means "ostrich mimic". It had no teeth in its beak and used its three-fingered hands to dig and grasp food. The tail helped it balance. Fossils were found in New Jersey and Canada.

Begin with the Bird Base (page 18).

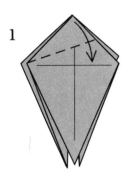

1

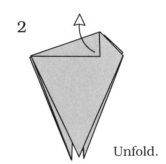

2

Unfold.

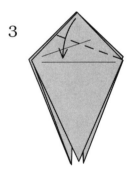

3

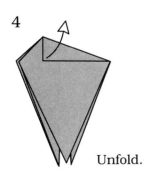

4

Unfold.

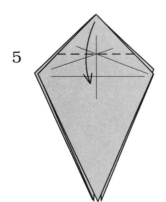

5

6

7

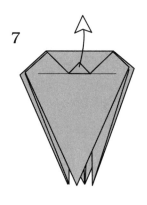

Unfold.

8

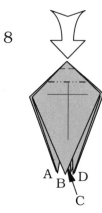

A B D
C

Sink down and up. Much of
the Bird Base will be unfolded.

9

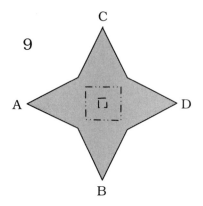

C

A   D

B

An intermediate step.

The Kuehneosaurus (page 29)
begins with this step.

10

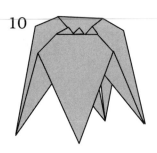

An intermediate step.

11

Repeat behind.

12

13

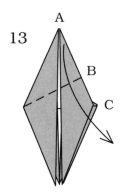

A

B

C

Fold down so that line A–B
touches corner C.

14

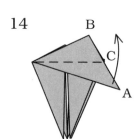

B

C

A

15

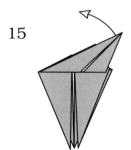

Unfold.

26   *Prehistoric Origami*

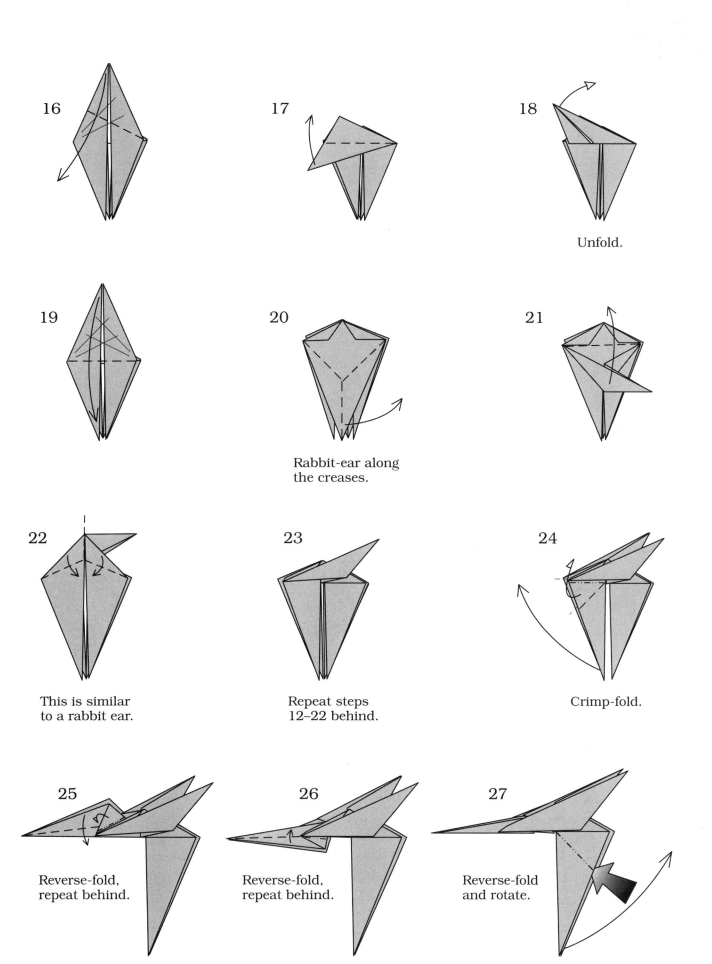

16

17

18

Unfold.

19

20

Rabbit-ear along
the creases.

21

22

This is similar
to a rabbit ear.

23

Repeat steps
12–22 behind.

24

Crimp-fold.

25

Reverse-fold,
repeat behind.

26

Reverse-fold,
repeat behind.

27

Reverse-fold
and rotate.

Struthiomimus 27

28

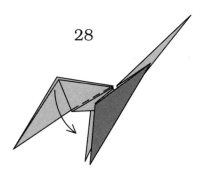

Fold under the dark
paper, repeat behind.

29

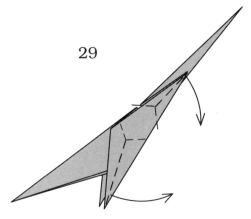

Rabbit-ear the arms and
legs, repeat behind.

30

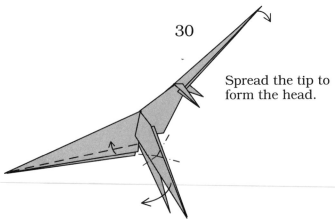

Spread the tip to
form the head.

Repeat behind.

31

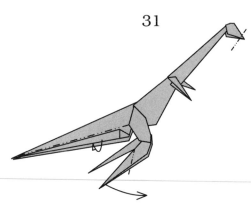

Fold the tip of the head inside.
Reverse-fold the hind legs. Thin
the tail and tuck the top inside
the center. Repeat behind.

32

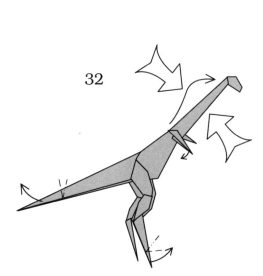

Curve the neck and tail.
Form hands and feet.
Repeat behind.

33

Struthiomimus

Kuehneosaurus

KU-nee-oh-saw-rus

This gliding lizard was 10 to 12 inches long and shared the Triassic period with some of the early dinosaurs. It probably climbed trees, spread its hollow ribs, and glided to earth. The ribs were covered with a thin skin. Insects were its favorite food.

Begin with step 12 of the Struthiomimus (page 25).

1

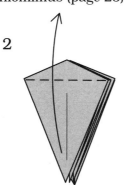

2

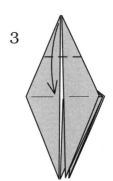

3

4

Unfold.

5

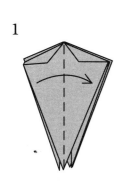

6

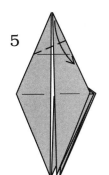

7

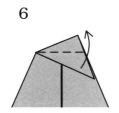

Unfold.

8

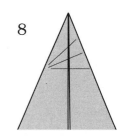

Repeat steps 5–7 in the opposite direction.

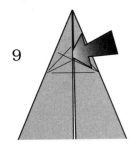

9

Place your finger here. In step 11, you will put your finger there to pull out some paper.

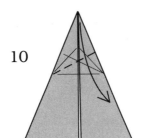

10

11

To pull out some paper, place your finger as shown in step 9.

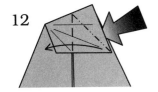

12

Squash-fold.

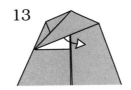

13

Pull out some paper.

14

15

Squash-fold.

16

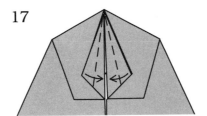

Petal-fold.

17

18

A
B
C

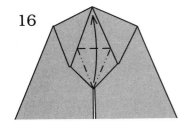

19

B
A
C

Reverse-fold repeat behind.

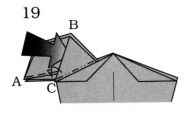

20

Reverse-fold repeat behind.

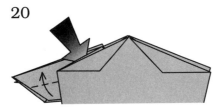

21

Squash-fold, repeat behind.

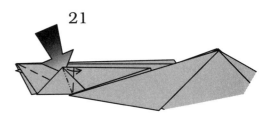

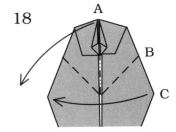

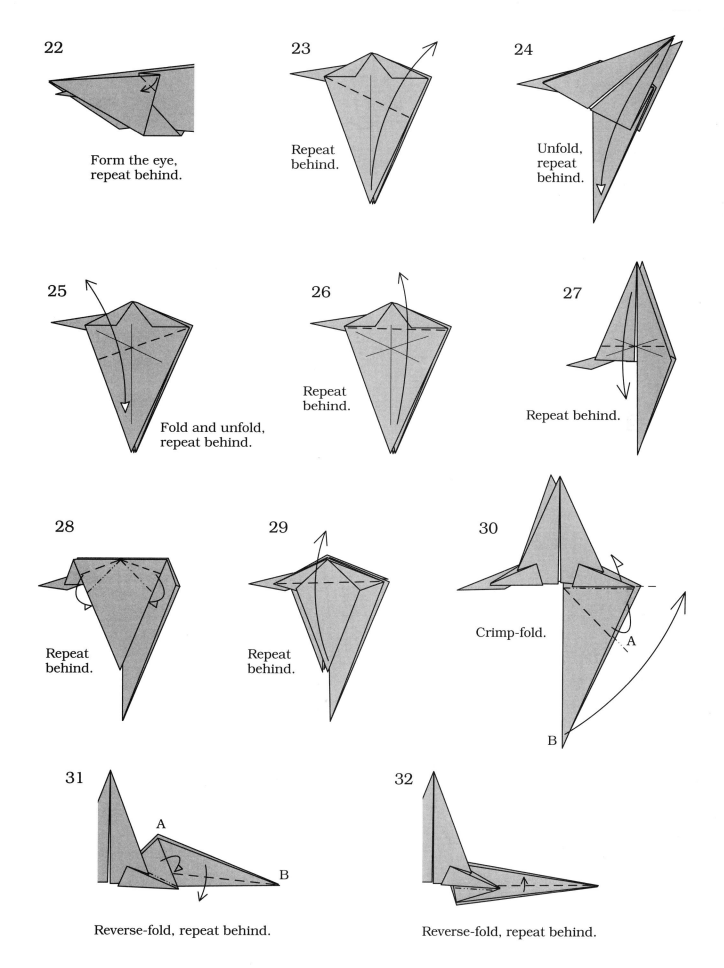

22

Form the eye, repeat behind.

23

Repeat behind.

24

Unfold, repeat behind.

25

Fold and unfold, repeat behind.

26

Repeat behind.

27

Repeat behind.

28

Repeat behind.

29

Repeat behind.

30

Crimp-fold.

A

B

31

A

B

Reverse-fold, repeat behind.

32

Reverse-fold, repeat behind.

33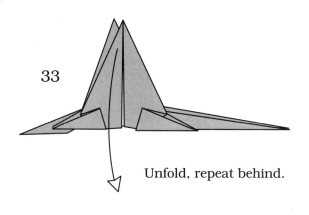

Unfold, repeat behind.

34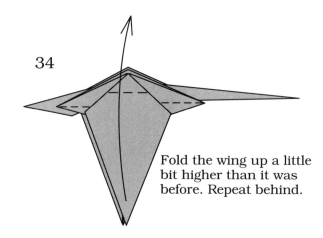

Fold the wing up a little bit higher than it was before. Repeat behind.

35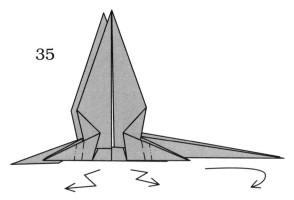

Curl the tail. Shape the legs, repeat behind.

36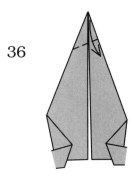

Repeat behind.

37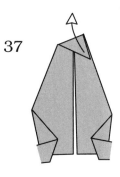

Unfold, repeat behind.

38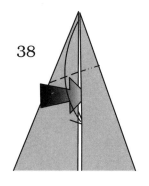

Tuck the tip inside, repeat behind.

39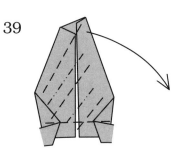

Repeat behind.

40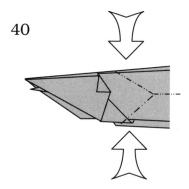

Sculp the head and neck by making it three-dimensional.

41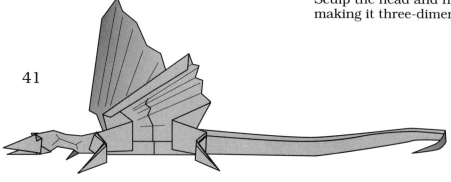

Kuehneosaurus

Archaeopteryx

are-key-OP-ter-ix

Once thought to be the first bird, this animal was more like a dinosaur than some of the Mesozoic animals that took to the air. It had solid bones, teeth in its beak, and was not able to fly or glide. It ran around the Jurassic forest floor catching insects. It was the size of a crow and was covered with feathers and scales. Archaeopteryx means "ancient wing".

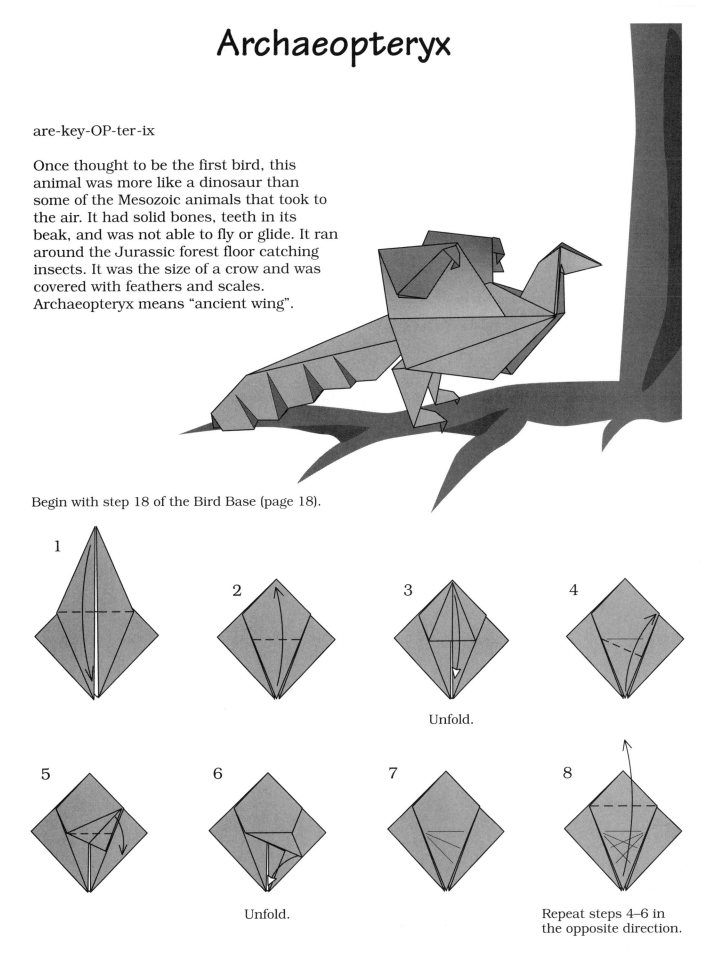

Begin with step 18 of the Bird Base (page 18).

1

2

3

4

Unfold.

5

6

Unfold.

7

8

Repeat steps 4–6 in the opposite direction.

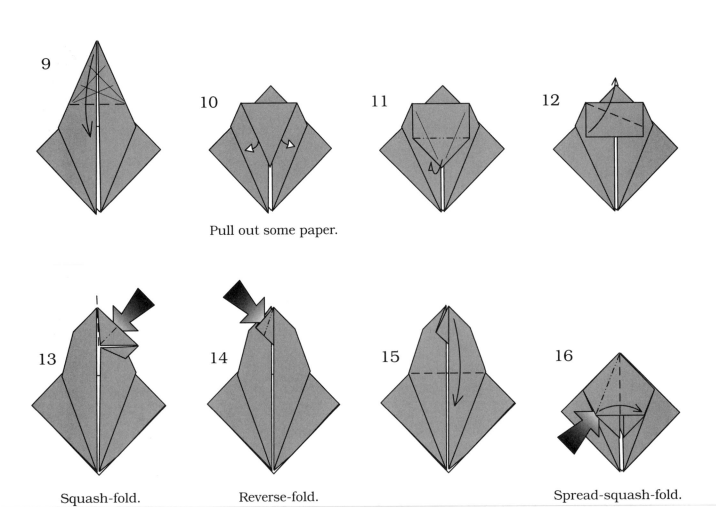

9

10

Pull out some paper.

11

12

13

Squash-fold.

14

Reverse-fold.

15

16

Spread-squash-fold.

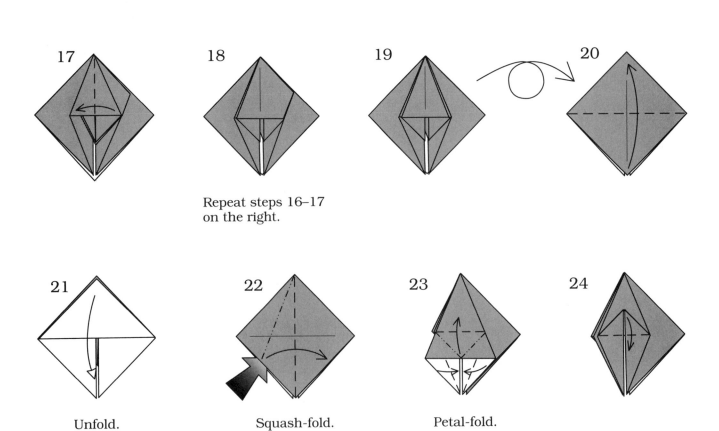

17

18

Repeat steps 16–17
on the right.

19

20

21

Unfold.

22

Squash-fold.

23

Petal-fold.

24

25

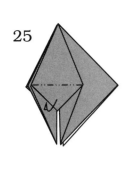

26

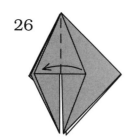

27

Repeat steps 22–26
on the right.

28

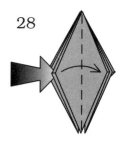

Fold two layers
to the right.

29

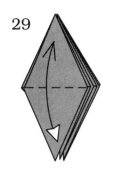

Fold up and unfold.

30

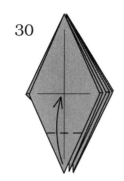

31

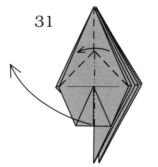

32

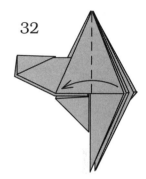

33

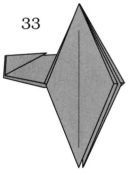

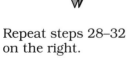

Repeat steps 28–32
on the right.

34

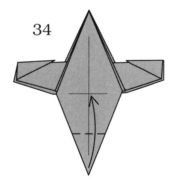

35

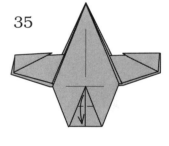

36

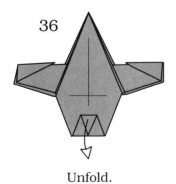

Unfold.

37

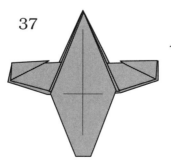

38

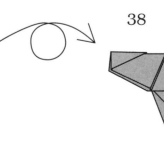

Unfold.

Archaeopteryx 35

39

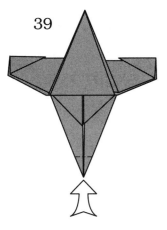

Fold the tip of
the tail inside.

40

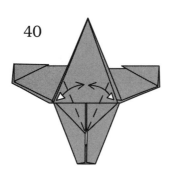

Kite-fold
and unfold.

41

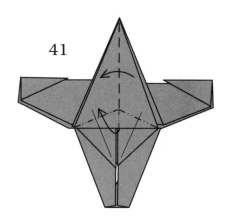

42

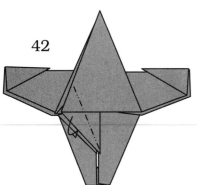

Repeat behind.

43

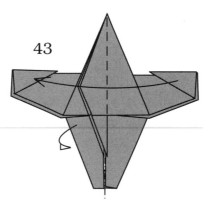

44

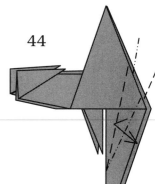

Crimp-fold.

45

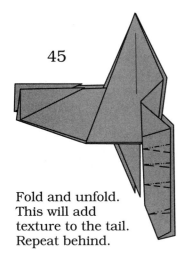

Fold and unfold.
This will add
texture to the tail.
Repeat behind.

46

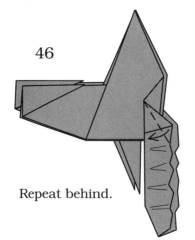

Repeat behind.

47

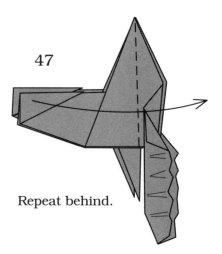

Repeat behind.

48

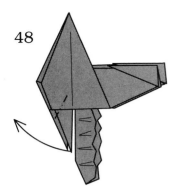

Reverse-fold.

49

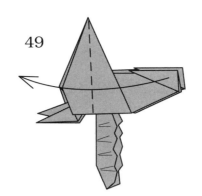

Repeat behind.

50

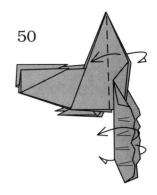

51

Repeat behind.

52

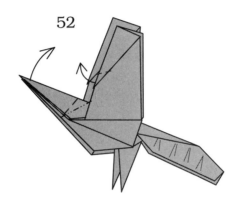

Crimp-fold the neck.
Outside-reverse-fold to form
the claws, repeat behind.

53

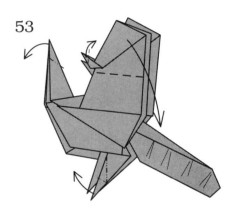

Repeat behind.

54 Head.

Fold two layers
down, repeat behind.

55 Foot.

Reverse-fold,
repeat behind.

56

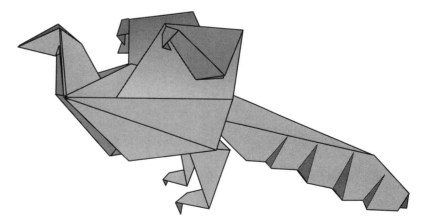

Archaeopteryx

Pterodactylus

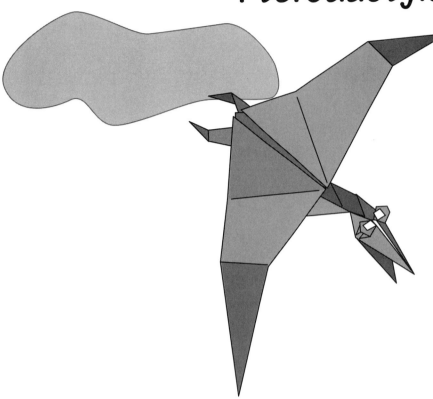

ter-oh-DAC-til-us

This tiny Jurassic reptile had an 18 inch wing span. It could have actually flapped its wings to fly. It ate insects and fish with its toothed beak. Fossils of Pterodactylus have been found in Europe.

Begin with the Bird Base (page 18).

1

2

Unfold.

3
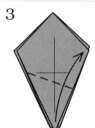

4
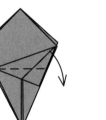

5
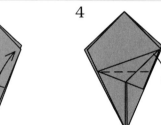

Unfold.

6

7
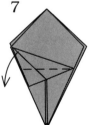

8

Unfold.

9

Repeat steps 1–8 behind. Skip this if you are folding the Quetzalcoatlus.

10
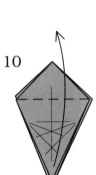

11

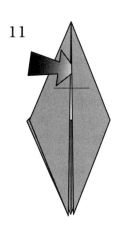

In step 13 you will
place your finger
inside here.

12

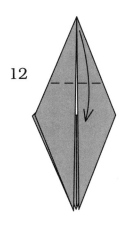

Fold along the
existing crease.

13

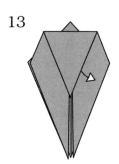

Pull out
some paper.

14

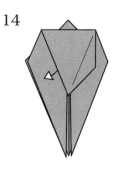

Pull out
some paper.

15

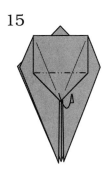

16

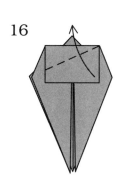

17

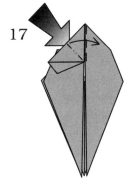

Squash-fold.

18

Squash-fold.

19

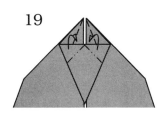

20

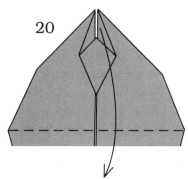

Return to step 28 of the
Quetzalcoatlus (page 43) if
you are folding it.

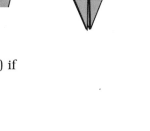

21

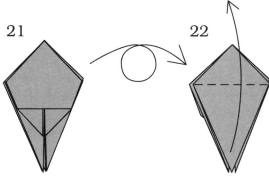

22

23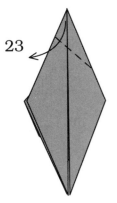

Fold on an
existing crease.

24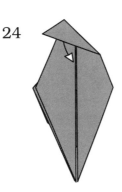

Pull out.

25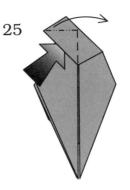

Squash-fold.

26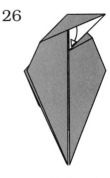

Pull out.

27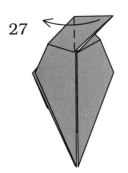

28

Squash-fold.

29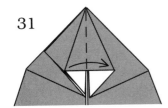

Fold up and unfold.

30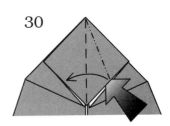

Squash-fold.

31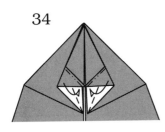

32

Repeat steps
30–31 on the left.

33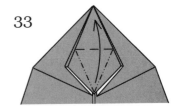

Petal-fold.

34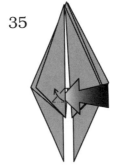

35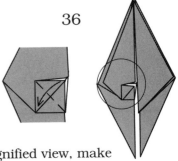

Squash-fold.

36

Magnified view, make
the eye white.

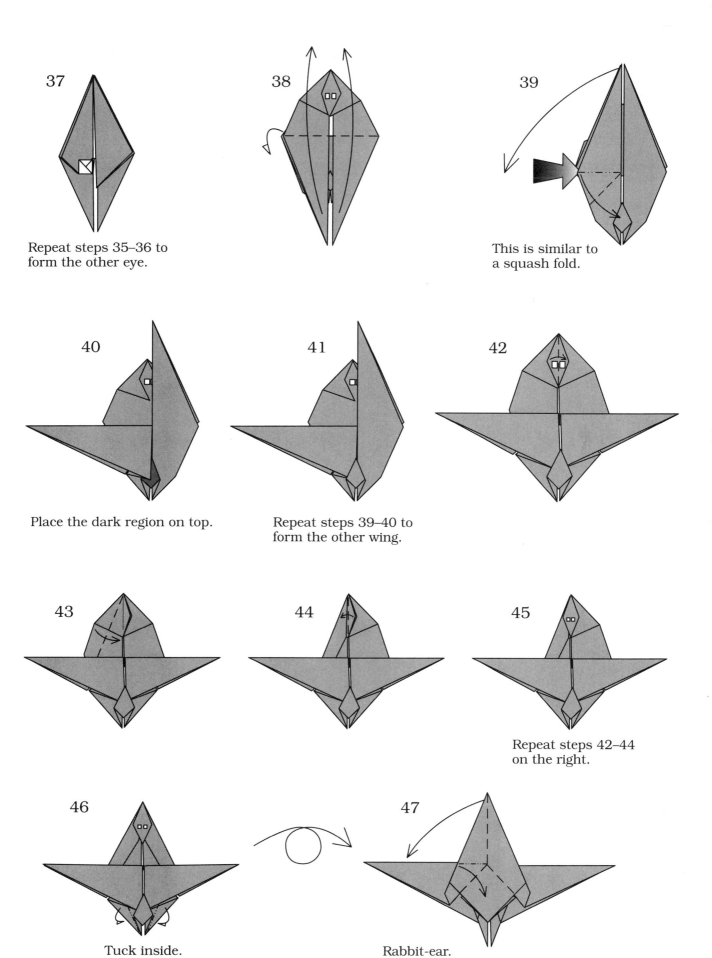

37

Repeat steps 35–36 to form the other eye.

38

39

This is similar to a squash fold.

40

Place the dark region on top.

41

Repeat steps 39–40 to form the other wing.

42

43

44

45

Repeat steps 42–44 on the right.

46

Tuck inside.

47

Rabbit-ear.

Pterodactylus 41

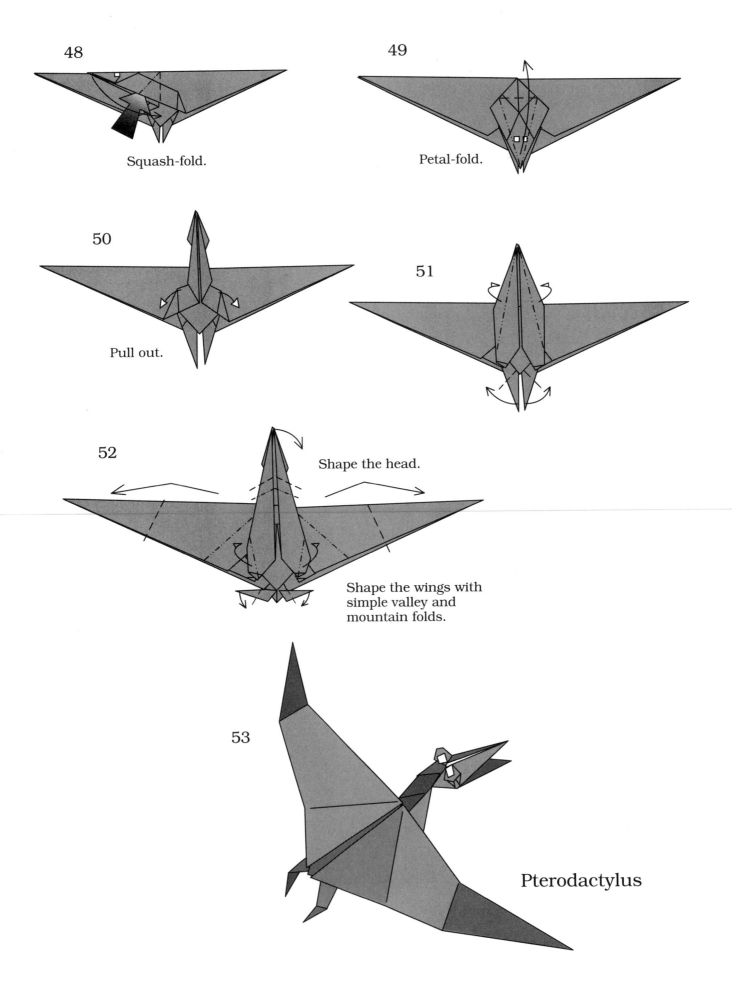

48

Squash-fold.

49

Petal-fold.

50

Pull out.

51

52

Shape the head.

Shape the wings with
simple valley and
mountain folds.

53

Pterodactylus

Quetzalcoatlus

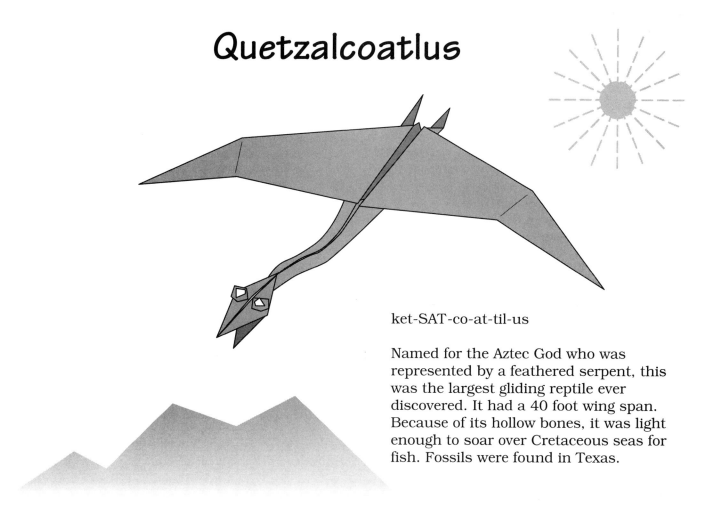

ket-SAT-co-at-til-us

Named for the Aztec God who was represented by a feathered serpent, this was the largest gliding reptile ever discovered. It had a 40 foot wing span. Because of its hollow bones, it was light enough to soar over Cretaceous seas for fish. Fossils were found in Texas.

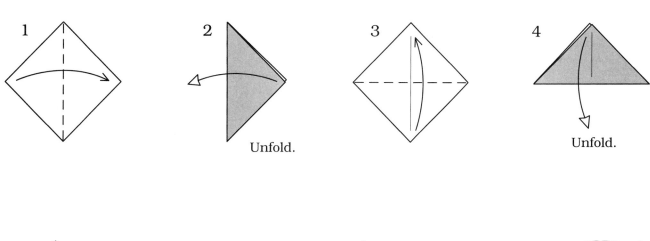

1

2

Unfold.

3

4

Unfold.

5

6

Unfold.

7

8

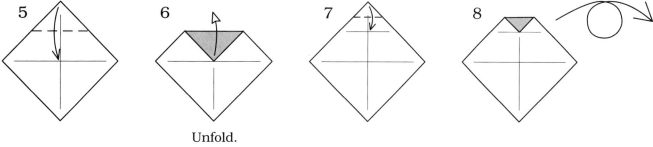

9

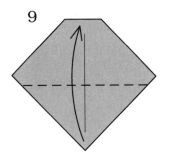

10

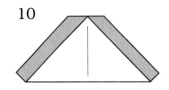

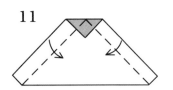

11

12

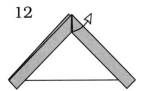

Pull out the corner.

13

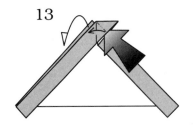

Squash-fold and fold
the back layer down.

14

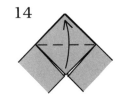

15

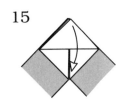

Unfold.

16

Squash-fold.

17

18

Repeat steps 16–17
on the left.

19

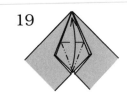

Petal-fold.

20

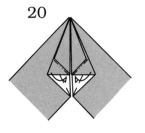

21

This will form
the head.

22

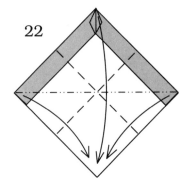

This is similar to the
Preliminary Fold.

23

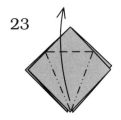

Petal-fold,
repeat behind.

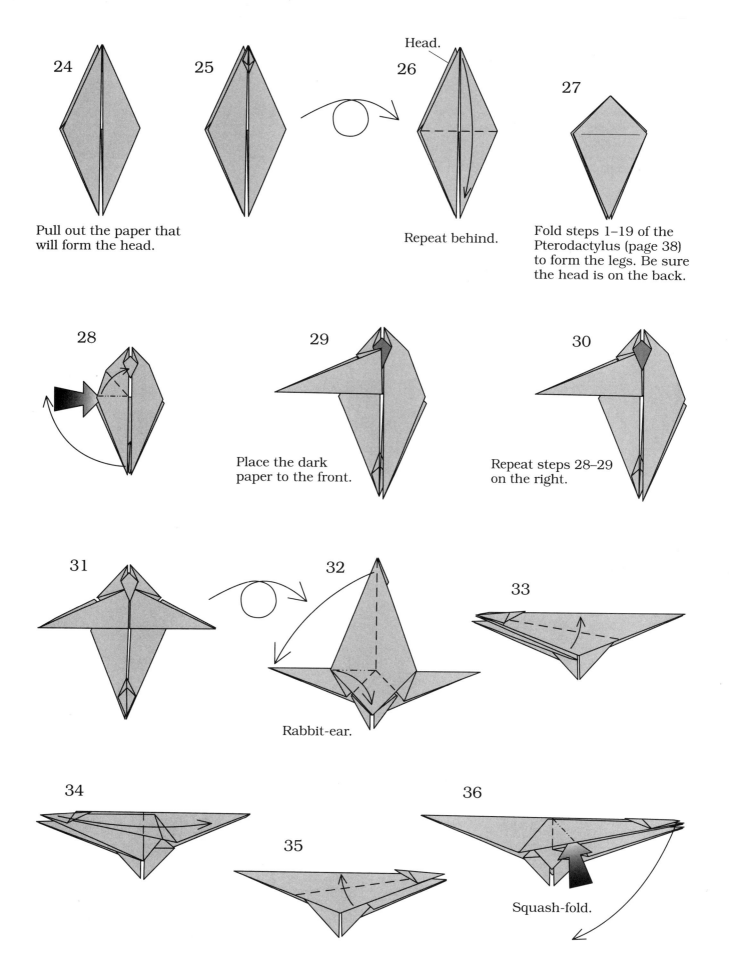

24

Pull out the paper that will form the head.

25

26

Head.

Repeat behind.

27

Fold steps 1–19 of the Pterodactylus (page 38) to form the legs. Be sure the head is on the back.

28

29

Place the dark paper to the front.

30

Repeat steps 28–29 on the right.

31

32

Rabbit-ear.

33

34

35

36

Squash-fold.

Quetzalcoatlus 45

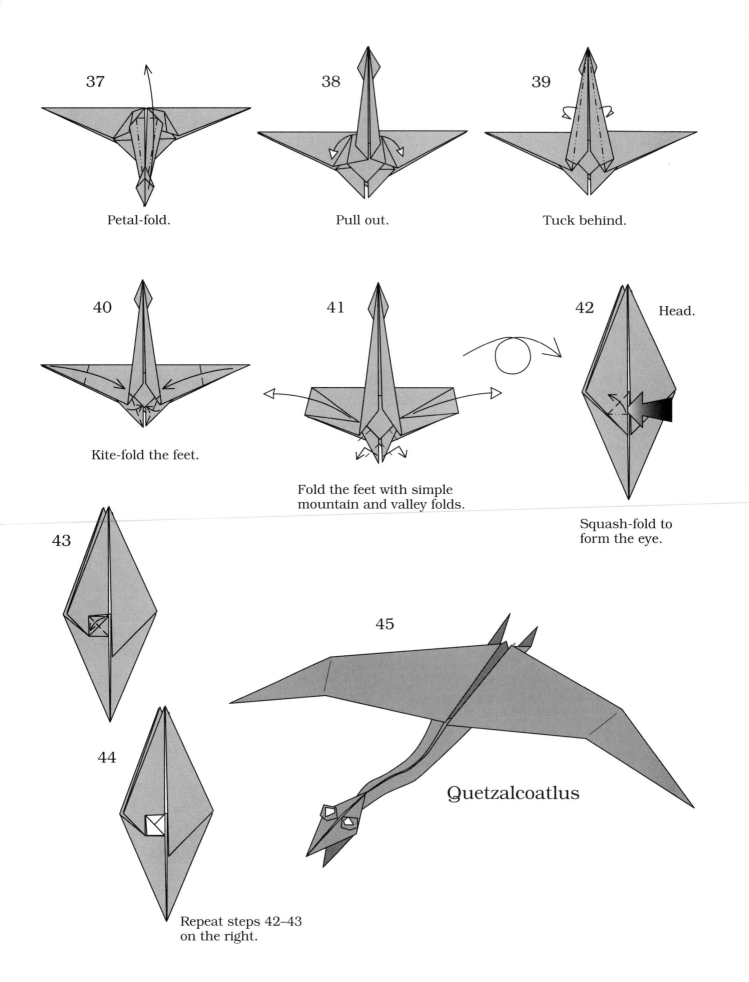

37

Petal-fold.

38

Pull out.

39

Tuck behind.

40

Kite-fold the feet.

41

Fold the feet with simple
mountain and valley folds.

42

Head.

Squash-fold to
form the eye.

43

44

Repeat steps 42–43
on the right.

45

Quetzalcoatlus

Frog Base

1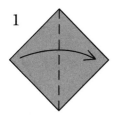

Fold in half.

2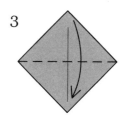

Unfold.

3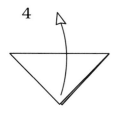

Fold in half.

4

Unfold.

5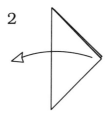

Turn over.

6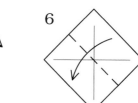

Book-fold.

7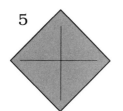

Unfold.

8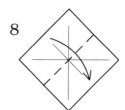

Book-fold.

9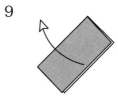

Unfold.

10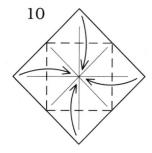

11

Unfold.

12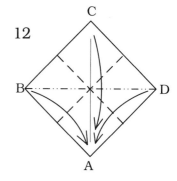

Collapse along the creases
so that corners B, C, and D
lie on top of A.

11

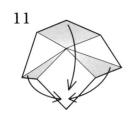

This is a
three-dimensional
intermediate step.

12

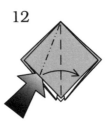

Squash-fold.

13

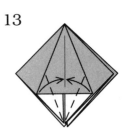

14

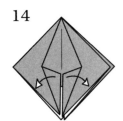

Unfold.

15

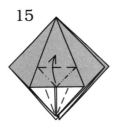

Petal-fold.

16

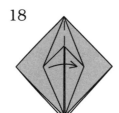

17

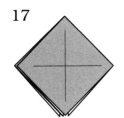

Repeat steps 12–15.

18

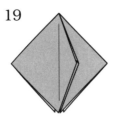

Repeat behind.

19

Repeat steps 12–15
in front and behind.

20

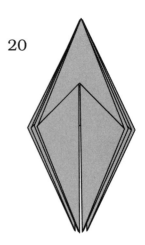

Frog Base

Rhamphorynchus

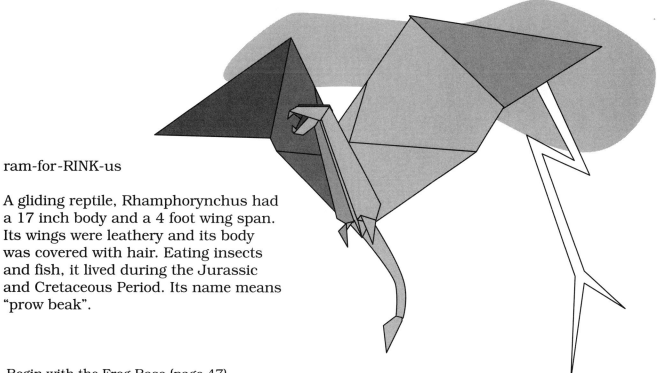

ram-for-RINK-us

A gliding reptile, Rhamphorynchus had a 17 inch body and a 4 foot wing span. Its wings were leathery and its body was covered with hair. Eating insects and fish, it lived during the Jurassic and Cretaceous Period. Its name means "prow beak".

Begin with the Frog Base (page 47).

1

2

3

An intermediate step.

4

Repeat steps 1–3 on the back and sides.

5

6

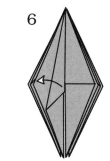

Unfold.

7

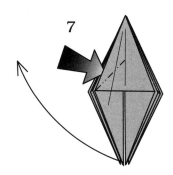

Reverse-fold.

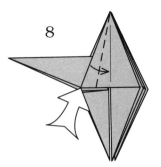

8

Spread-squash-fold.

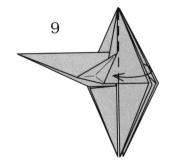

9

Fold two layers
to the left.

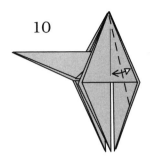

10

Fold and unfold.

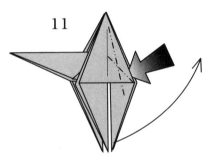

11

Reverse-fold.

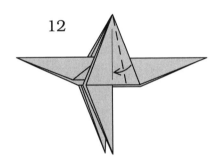

12

Spread-squash-fold.

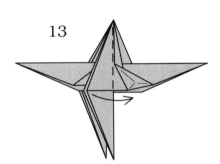

13

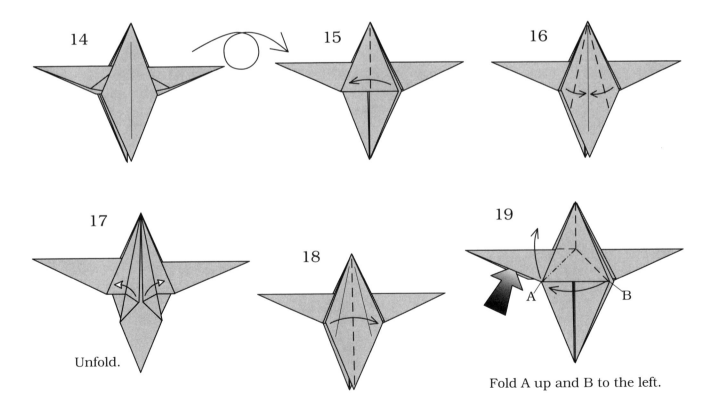

14

15

16

17

Unfold.

18

19

A   B

Fold A up and B to the left.

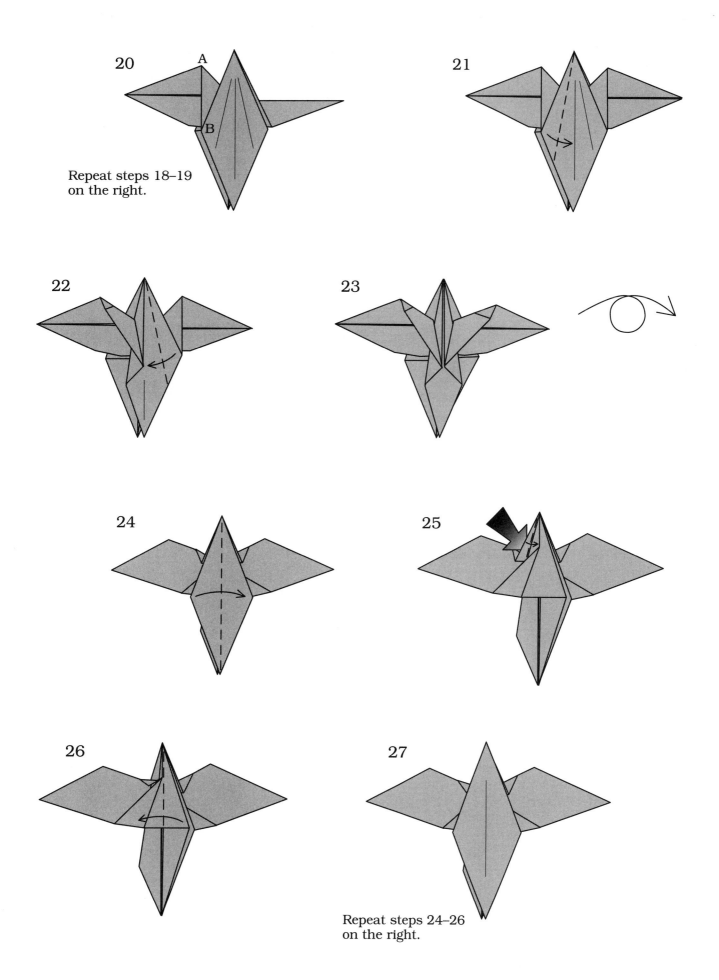

20

A

B

Repeat steps 18–19
on the right.

21

22

23

24

25

26

27

Repeat steps 24–26
on the right.

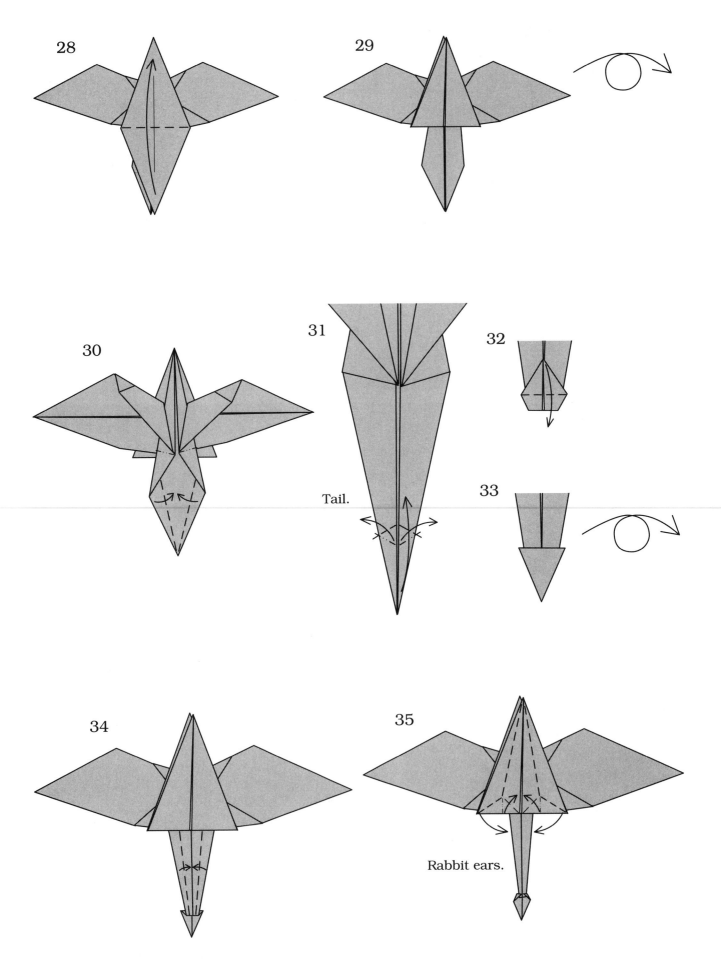

28

29

30

31

Tail.

32

33

34

35

Rabbit ears.

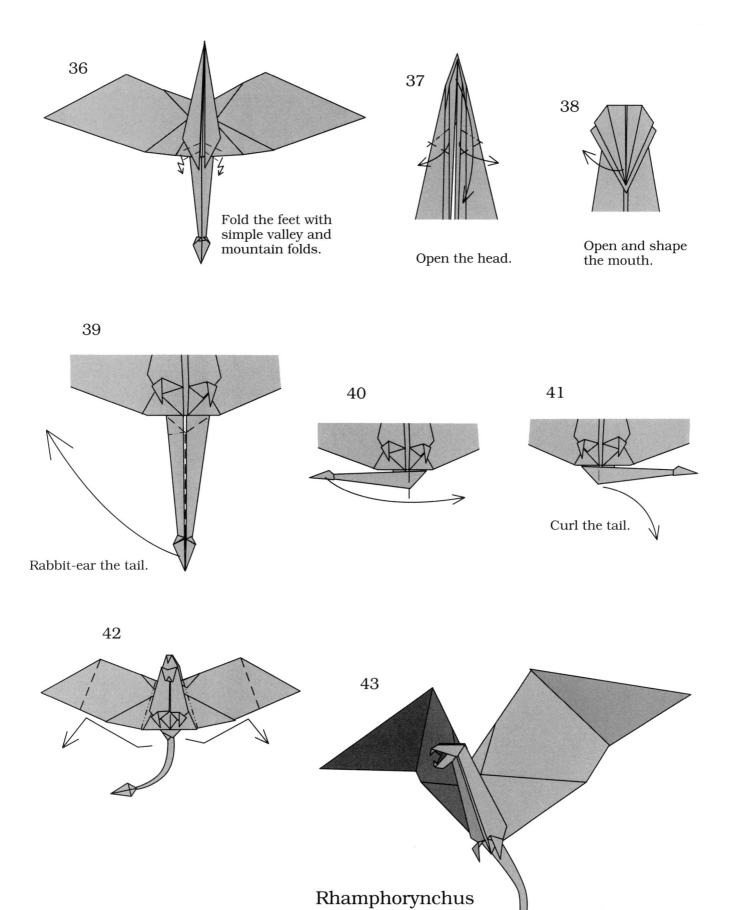

36

Fold the feet with simple valley and mountain folds.

37

Open the head.

38

Open and shape the mouth.

39

Rabbit-ear the tail.

40

41

Curl the tail.

42

43

Rhamphorynchus

Pteranodon

ter-RAN-oh-don

With a 20 foot wing span, this gliding reptile swooped over Cretaceous seas picking up fish to eat. Its name means "toothless wing". The skin stretching across its "wings" was probably covered with hair. It glided off ocean cliffs in the western U.S.

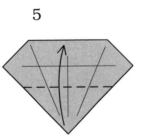

1

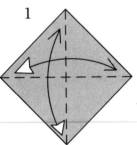

Fold and unfold along the diagonals.

2

Kite-fold.

3

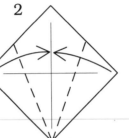

Unfold.

4

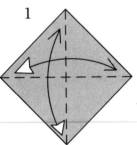

5

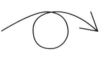

6

7

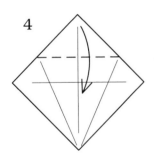

8

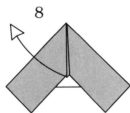

Pull out the hidden corner.

9

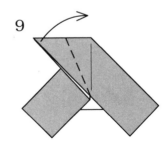

10

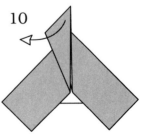

Unfold.

11

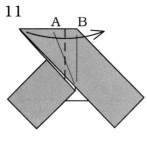

A B

Fold A to B.

12

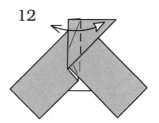

Fold and unfold.

13

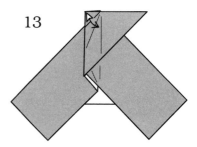

Fold and unfold.

14

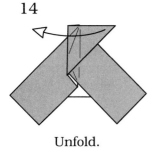

Unfold.

15

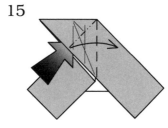

Squash-fold.

16

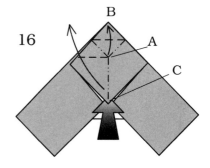

B

A

C

Fold A to B while folding
C up and to the left.

17

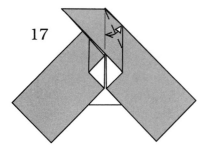

Fold along the crease
line and unfold.

18

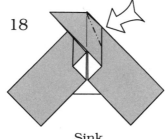

Sink.

19

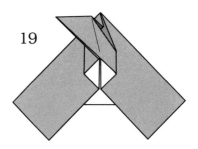

A three-dimensional
intermediate step.

20

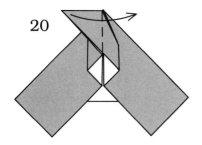

21

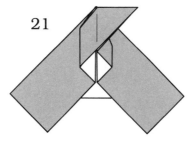

Repeat steps 17–19
on the left.

22

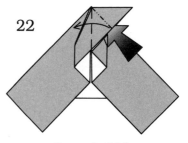

Squash-fold.

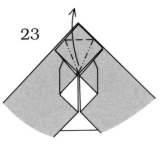

23

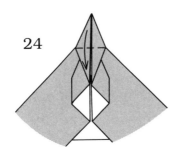

24

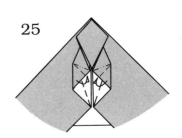

25

Petal-fold.

26

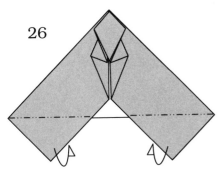

Fold inside.

27

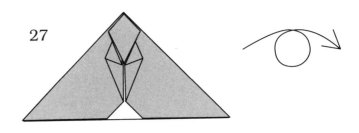

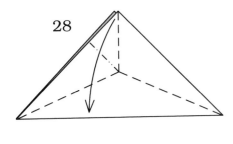

28

Rabbit-ear.

29

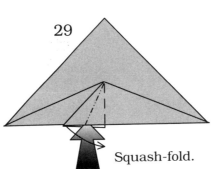

Squash-fold.

30

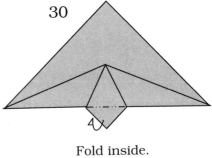

Fold inside.

31

32

33

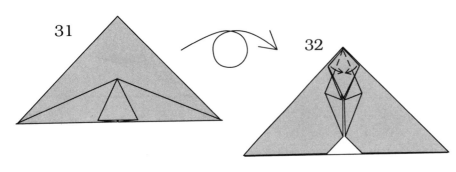

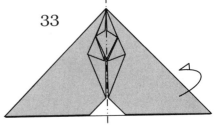

34

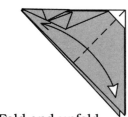

Fold and unfold,
repeat behind.

35

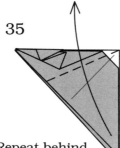

Repeat behind.

36

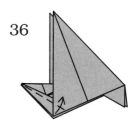

Fold at an angle of
one-third, repeat behind.

37

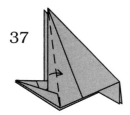

Repeat behind.

38

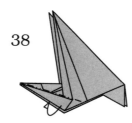

Repeat behind.

39

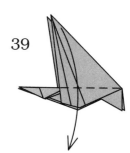

Repeat behind.

40

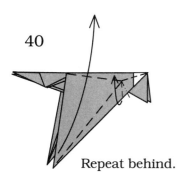

Repeat behind.

41

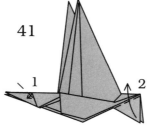

Repeat behind.

42

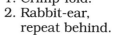

1. Crimp-fold.
2. Rabbit-ear,
   repeat behind.

43

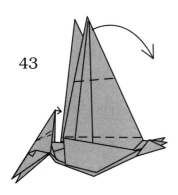

Repeat behind.

44

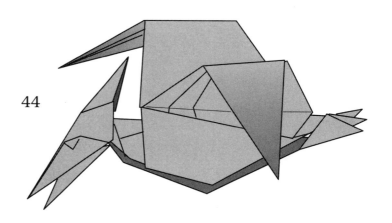

Pteranodon

Elasmosaurus

e-LAZ-mo-saw-rus

This marine reptile's name means "ribbon lizard". It was 40 feet long with as many as 76 bones in its neck. Fossils have been found in Kansas which was a shallow sea in the Cretaceous Period. It used its long neck and sharp teeth to dine on fish.

1

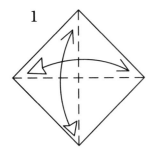

Fold and unfold along the diagonals.

2

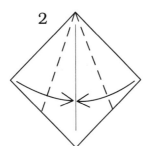

Kite-fold.

3

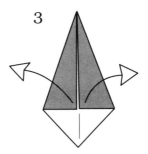

Unfold.

4

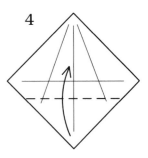

Fold and unfold.

5

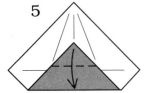

6

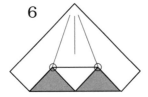

If all the lines intersect where the circles are drawn then continue. Otherwise, repeat steps 4–5.

7

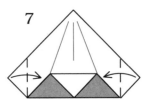

8

Unfold.

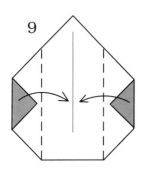

9

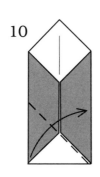

10

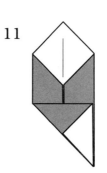

11

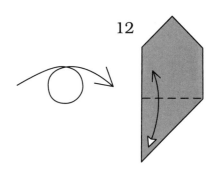

12

Fold up and unfold.

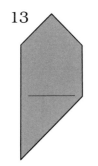

13

14

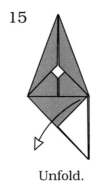

15

Unfold.

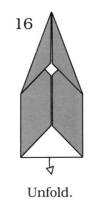

16

Unfold.

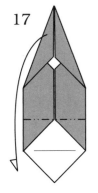

17

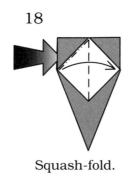

18

Squash-fold.

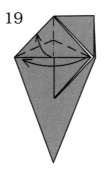

19

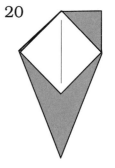

20

Repeat steps 18–19 on the right.

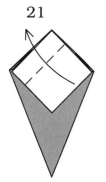

21

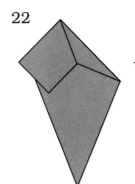

22

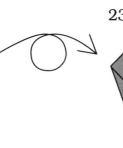

23

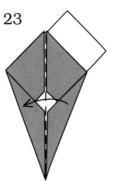

24

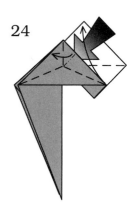

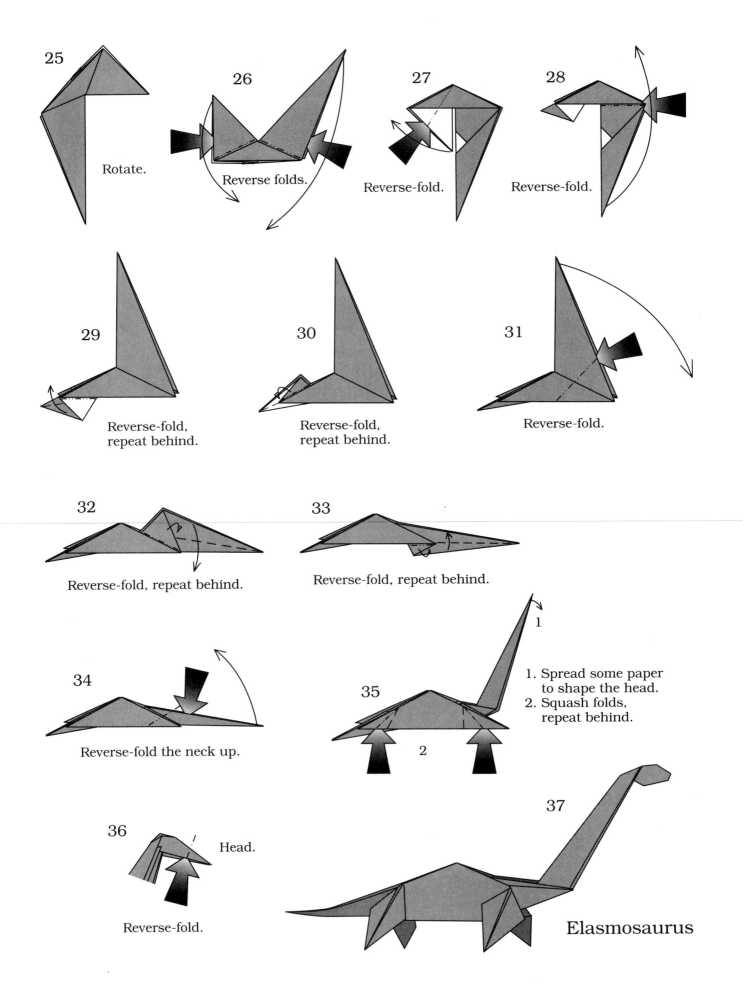

25

Rotate.

26

Reverse folds.

27

Reverse-fold.

28

Reverse-fold.

29

Reverse-fold,
repeat behind.

30

Reverse-fold,
repeat behind.

31

Reverse-fold.

32

Reverse-fold, repeat behind.

33

Reverse-fold, repeat behind.

34

Reverse-fold the neck up.

35

1
2

1. Spread some paper
to shape the head.
2. Squash folds,
repeat behind.

36

Head.

Reverse-fold.

37

Elasmosaurus

Tanystropheus

tan-e-STRO-fee-us

This lizard lived on the shores of Triassic seas in Germany. The hip structure clearly prevents it from being called a dinosaur. Its 9 foot long neck was more than half its total 15 foot length. It could remain on the shore and fish for food beneath the surface of the water.

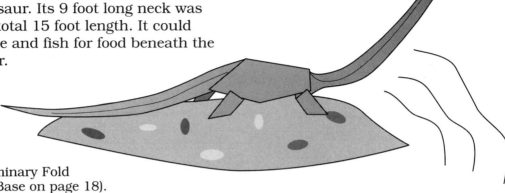

Begin with the Preliminary Fold (step 12 of the Bird Base on page 18).

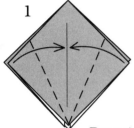

1

Repeat behind.

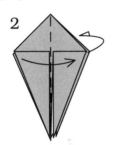

2

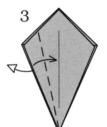

3

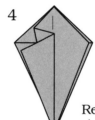

4

Repeat step 3 on the right and behind.

5

Fold down and unfold.

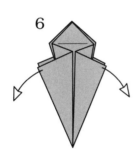

6

Unfold, repeat behind.

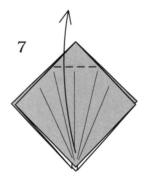

7

Begin a thin petal fold.

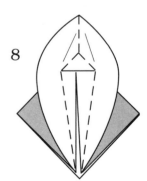

8

This is a three dimensional figure.

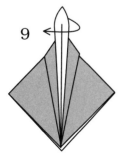

9

This is a three dimensional figure.

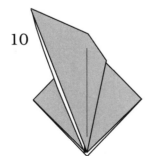

10

Repeat steps 7–9 behind.

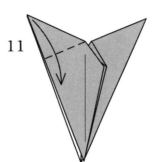

11

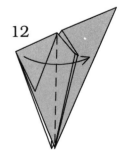

12

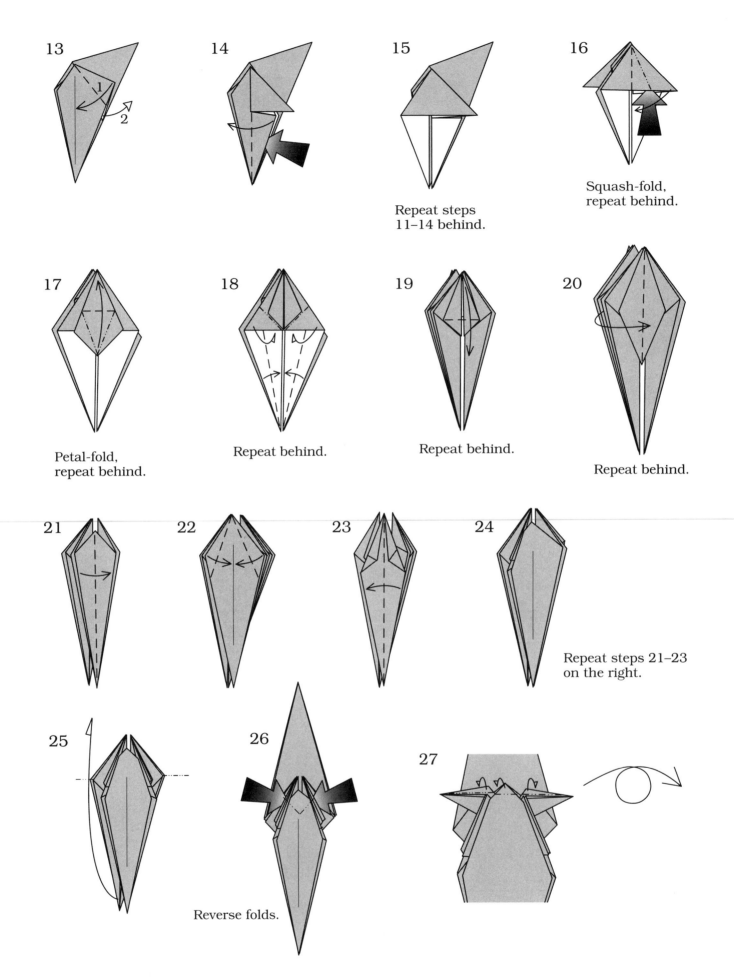

13

14

15

Repeat steps
11–14 behind.

16

Squash-fold,
repeat behind.

17

Petal-fold,
repeat behind.

18

Repeat behind.

19

Repeat behind.

20

Repeat behind.

21

22

23

24

Repeat steps 21–23
on the right.

25

26

Reverse folds.

27

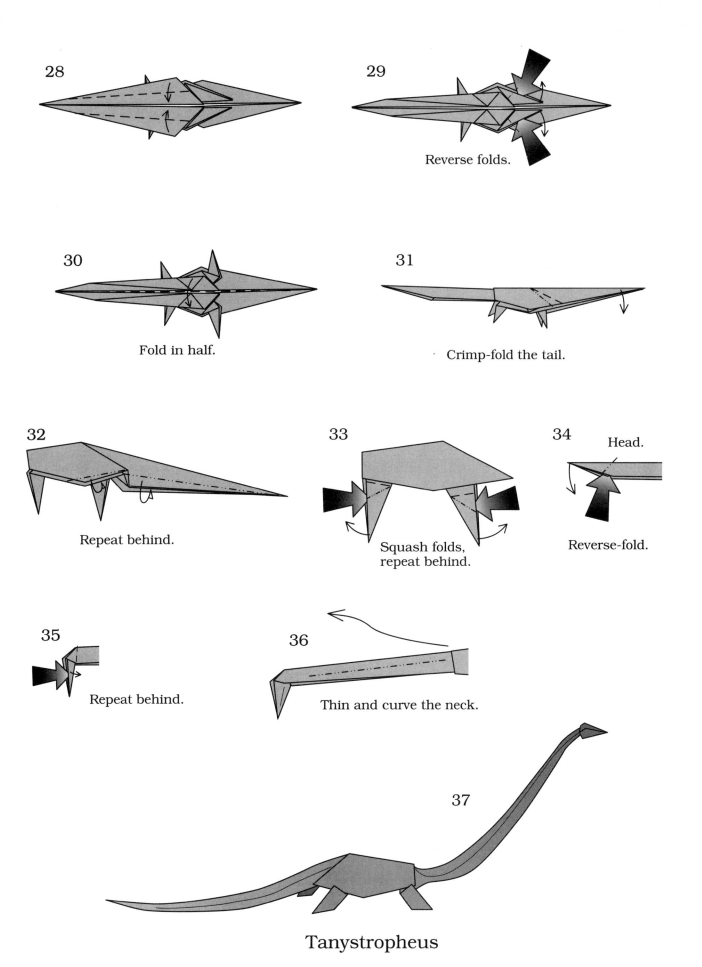

28

29

Reverse folds.

30

Fold in half.

31

Crimp-fold the tail.

32

Repeat behind.

33

Squash folds,
repeat behind.

34

Head.

Reverse-fold.

35

Repeat behind.

36

Thin and curve the neck.

37

Tanystropheus

Apatosaurus

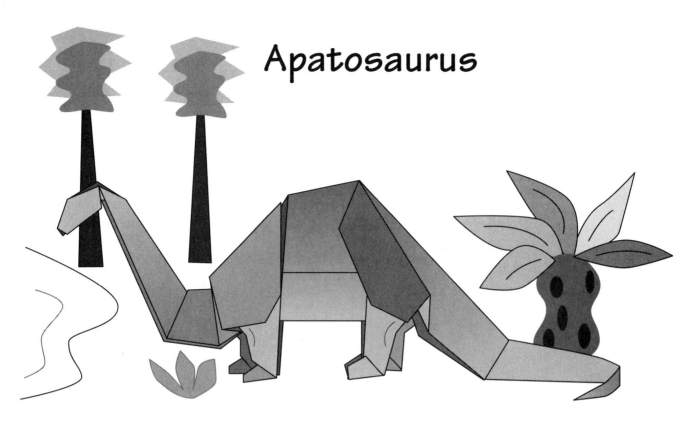

a-PAT-oh-saw-rus

This dinosaur is better known as Brontosaurus, the "thunder lizard" but more correctly named Apatosaurus, the "headless lizard". It was 70 feet long and very heavy. The front legs were shorter than the back legs. Its fossils were found in the western U.S. with other Jurassic dinosaurs. Its small flat teeth could not have ground up all the food required to fuel this animal so it relied on "gizzard stones" to aid in digestion.

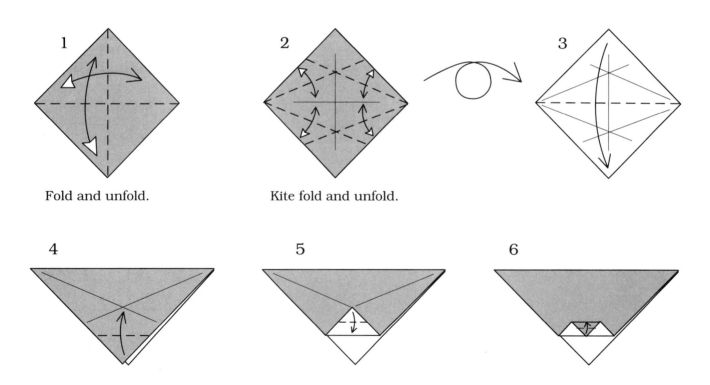

1

Fold and unfold.

2

Kite fold and unfold.

3

4

5

6

7

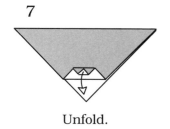

Unfold.

8

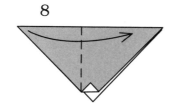

9

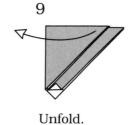

Unfold.

10

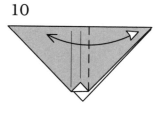

Fold to the left
and unfold.

11

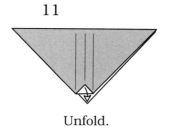

Unfold.

12

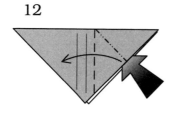

Squash fold.

13

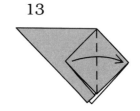

14

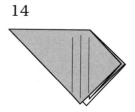

Repeat steps
12–13 on the left.

15

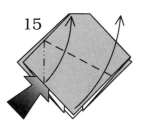

Squash fold.

16

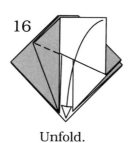

Unfold.

17

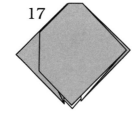

Repeat steps 15–16 on
the right and back.

18

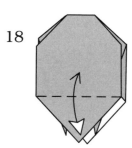

Fold up and unfold.
Repeat behind.

19

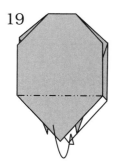

Repeat behind.

20

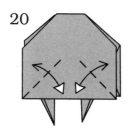

Fold and unfold.
Repeat behind.

21

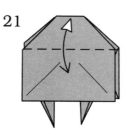

Fold down
and unfold.

22

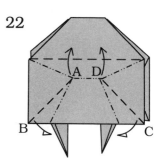

This is a tricky fold!
Lift A–D up while
bringing B and C
closer together.

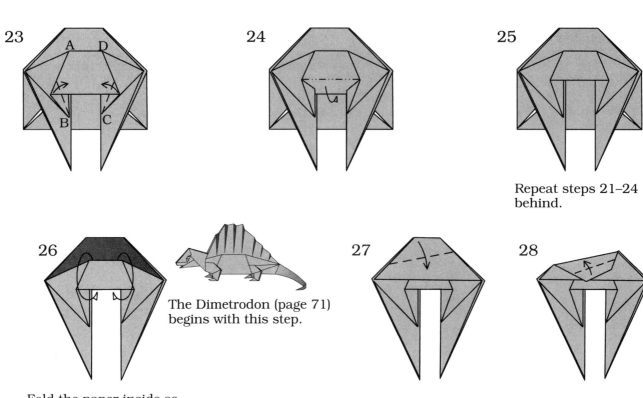

23

24

25

Repeat steps 21–24 behind.

26

Fold the paper inside so the darker region will be on top. Repeat behind.

The Dimetrodon (page 71) begins with this step.

27

28

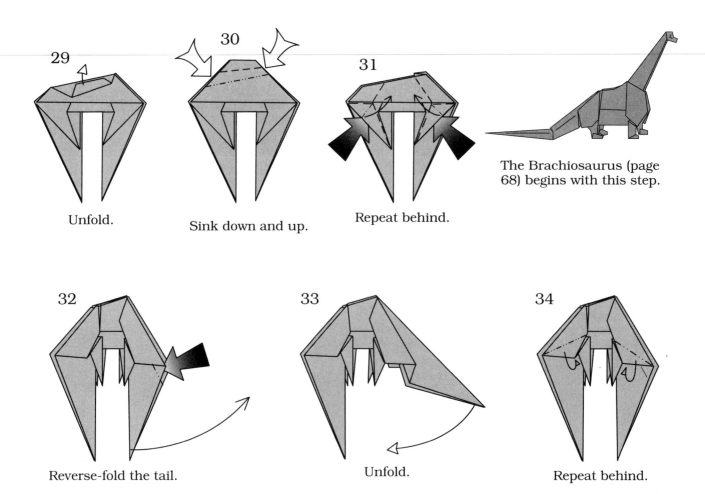

29

Unfold.

30

Sink down and up.

31

Repeat behind.

The Brachiosaurus (page 68) begins with this step.

32

Reverse-fold the tail.

33

Unfold.

34

Repeat behind.

35

Repeat behind.

36

Reverse-folds.

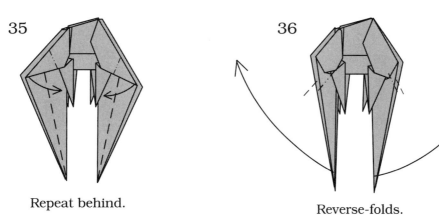

37

Crimp folds.

38

Head.

Reverse-fold.

39

Spread the head
while folding it down.

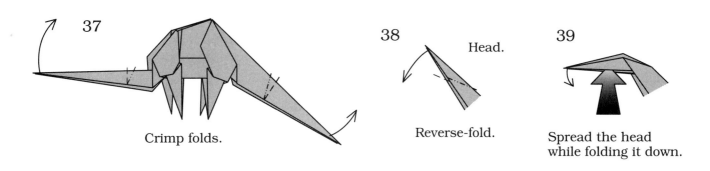

Front legs.

Hind legs.

40

Reverse-fold.

41

Repeat behind.

42

Repeat behind.

43

Repeat behind.

44

Repeat behind.

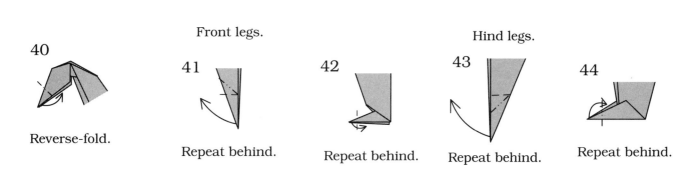

45

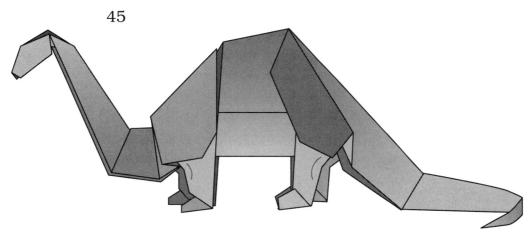

Apatosaurus

Brachiosaurus

BRAKE-ee-oh-saw-rus

This 75 foot long, Jurassic dinosaur was called "arm lizard" because its front legs were longer than its back legs. The placement of the nose on top of its head was once thought to aid in breathing when submerged in deep water. Now some paleontologists believe it lived on high ground, eating pine needles, since the skeleton could not have withstood the pressre of deep water. Fossils were found in Colorado.

Begin with step 31 of the Apatosaurus (page 64).

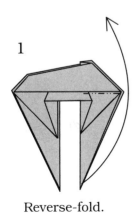

1

Reverse-fold.

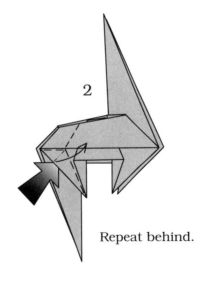

2

Repeat behind.

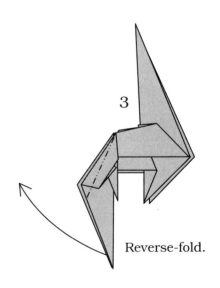

3

Reverse-fold.

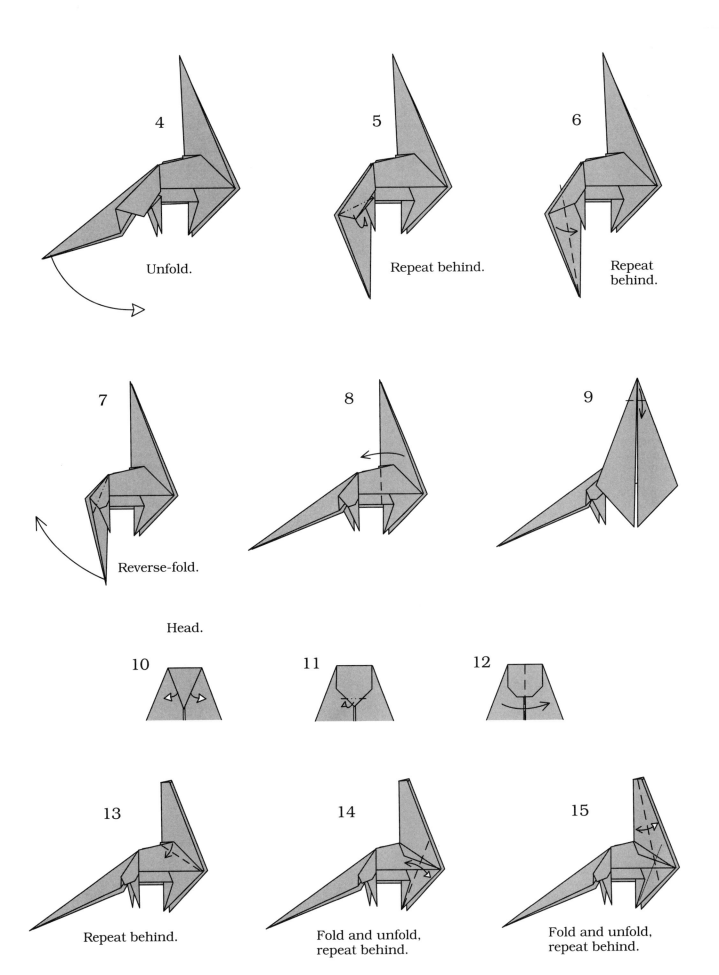

4

Unfold.

5

Repeat behind.

6

Repeat
behind.

7

Reverse-fold.

Head.

8

9

10

11

12

13

Repeat behind.

14

Fold and unfold,
repeat behind.

15

Fold and unfold,
repeat behind.

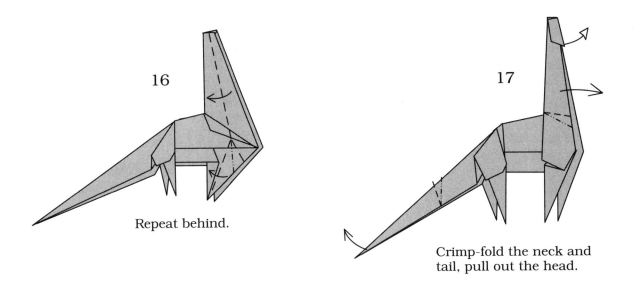

16

Repeat behind.

17

Crimp-fold the neck and tail, pull out the head.

Front leg.

18

Repeat behind.

19

Repeat behind.

Hind leg.

20

Repeat behind.

21

Repeat behind.

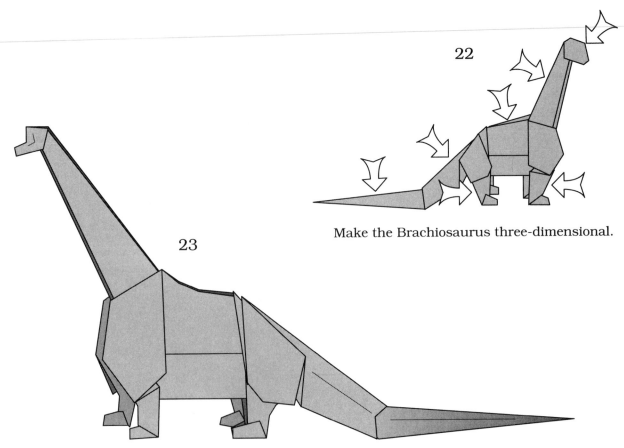

22

Make the Brachiosaurus three-dimensional.

23

Brachiosaurus

Dimetrodon

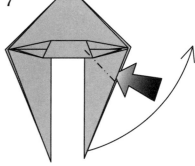

di-ME-tro-don

This was a very powerful meat eating reptile. Its name means "double measure tooth" because of its many knife-like teeth. It lived in the Permian Period immediately preceding the Mesozoic Era. It was about 10 feet long and the "sail" on its back helped regulate its body temperature.

Begin with step 26 of the Apatosaurus (page 64).

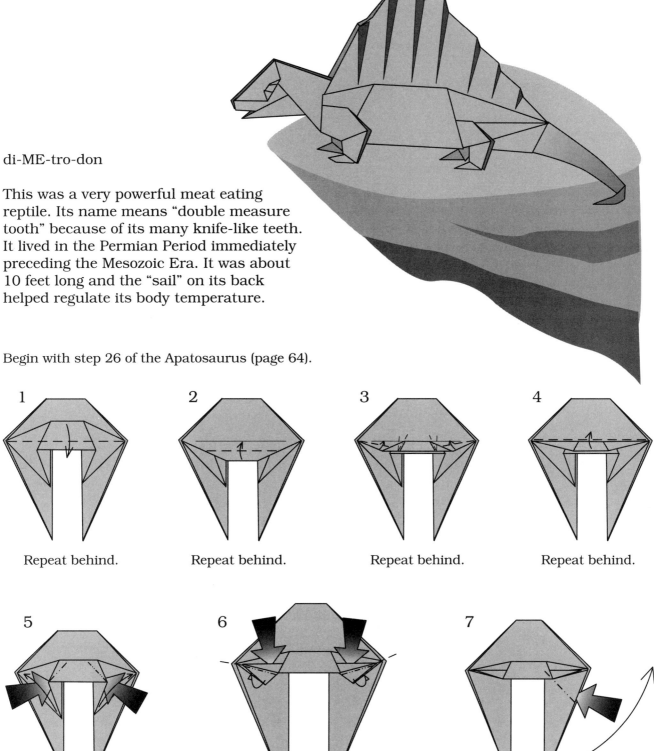

1

Repeat behind.

2

Repeat behind.

3

Repeat behind.

4

Repeat behind.

5

Reverse folds, repeat behind.

6

Reverse folds, repeat behind.

7

Reverse-fold.

8 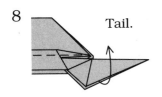 Tail.

9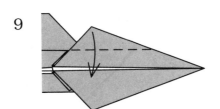

10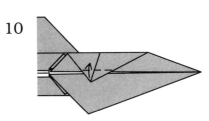

11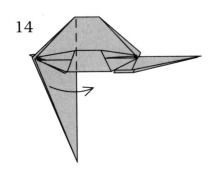

12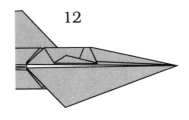

Repeat steps 9–11.

13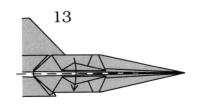

14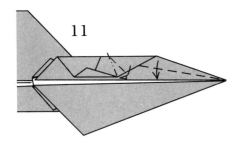

15 Head.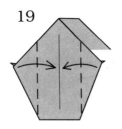

16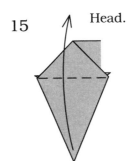

17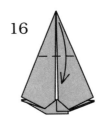

18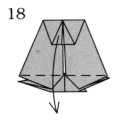

19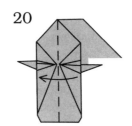

20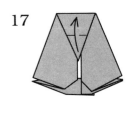

21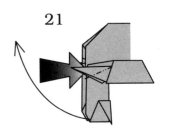

Reverse-fold.

22

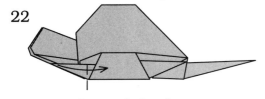

Repeat behind.

23

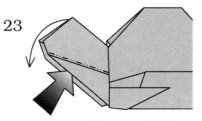

Reverse-fold.

24

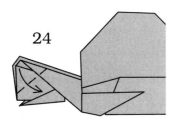

Repeat behind.

25

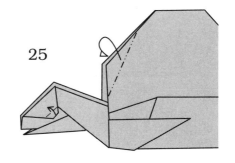

Form the eye and shape
the back. Repeat behind.

26

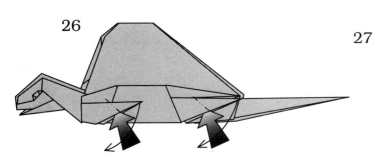

Reverse folds, repeat behind.

27

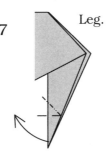

Leg.

Crimp-fold the four legs.

28

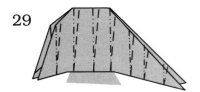

Crimp-fold and curl the tail.

29

Pleat Dimetrodon's sail.

30

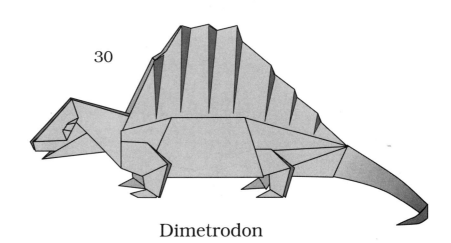

Dimetrodon

Spinosaurus

SPINE-oh-saw-rus

This 40 foot long dinosaur was a fierce meat eater. The sail down its back helped control its body heat. Fossils were found in Egypt. It lived at the end of the Cretaceous Period. Spinosaurus means "spine lizard". Despite the sail, Spinosaurus was not related to Dimetrodon.

1
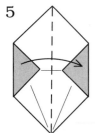
Fold and unfold.

2
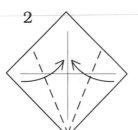

3
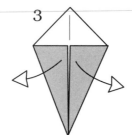
Unfold.

4
A   B
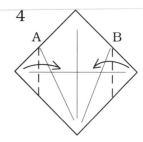
Use the points A and B as guides.

5
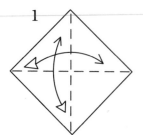

6

7

Unfold.

8
B
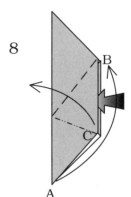
C
A
Squash-fold.

9

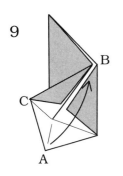

This is a three-dimensional intermediate step.

10

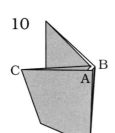

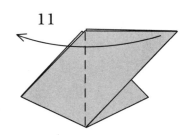

Turn over and rotate.

11

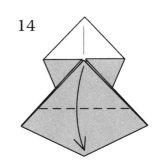

12

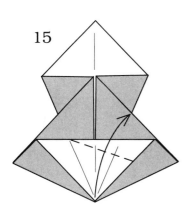

Squash-fold.

13

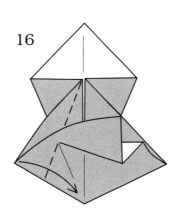

14

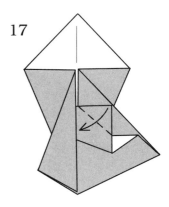

15

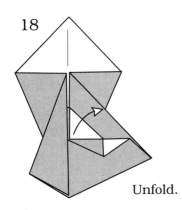

16

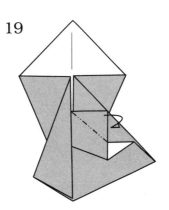

This is a three-dimensional intermediate step.

17

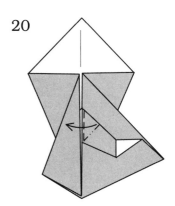

18

Unfold.

19

20

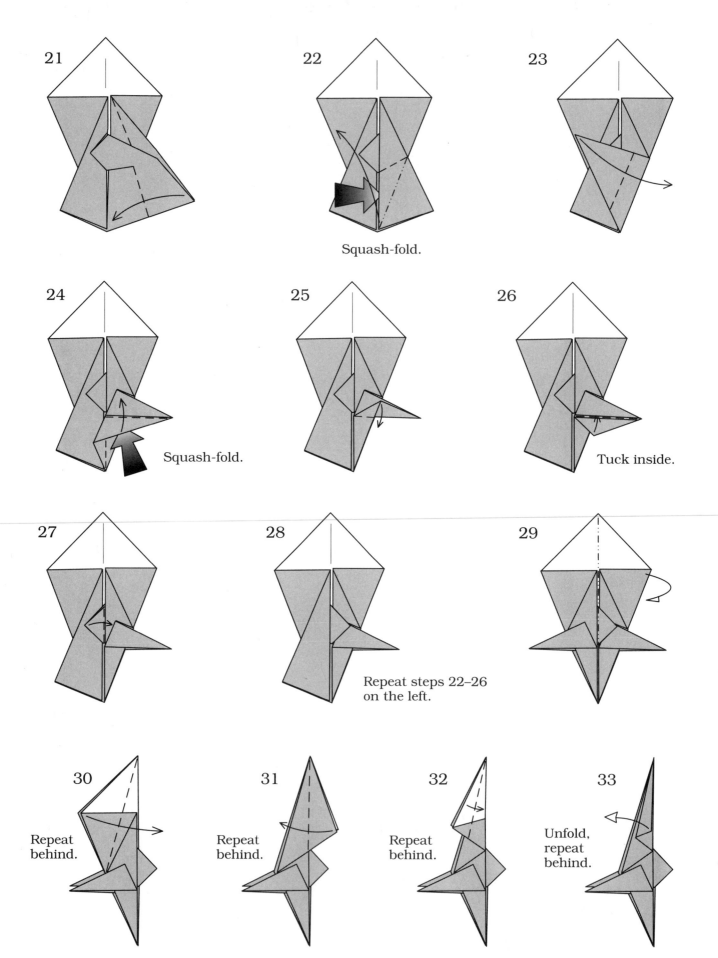

21

22

Squash-fold.

23

24

Squash-fold.

25

26

Tuck inside.

27

28

Repeat steps 22–26
on the left.

29

30

Repeat
behind.

31

Repeat
behind.

32

Repeat
behind.

33

Unfold,
repeat
behind.

34

35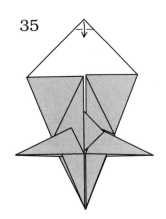

36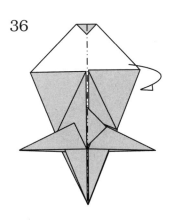

37

Reverse-fold,
repeat behind.

38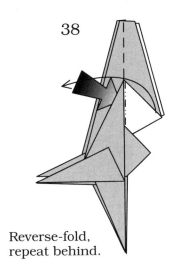

Reverse-fold,
repeat behind.

39

Reverse-fold,
repeat behind.

40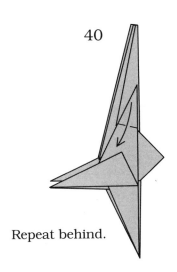

Repeat behind.

41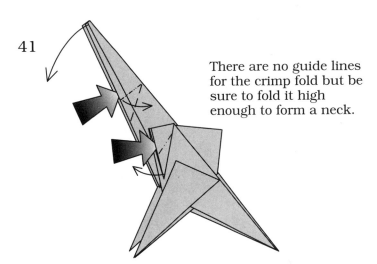

There are no guide lines
for the crimp fold but be
sure to fold it high
enough to form a neck.

Crimp-fold the neck and reverse-fold
the arm, repeat behind.

42

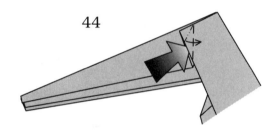

1. Pull out.
2. Reverse-fold.
3. Crimp-fold.
Repeat behind.

43

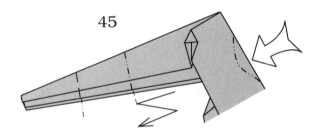

Repeat behind.

Curl the tail.

44

Form the eye with a squash
fold, repeat behind.

45

Form the mouth with a crimp fold.
Shape the neck.

46

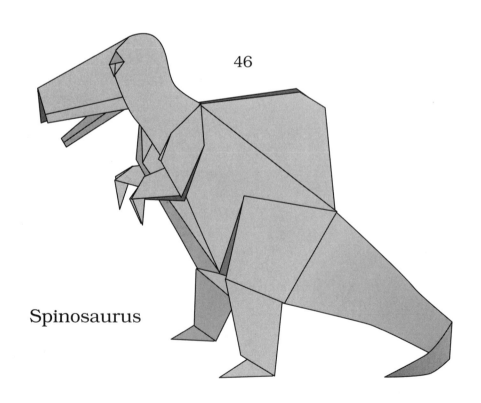

Spinosaurus

Tyrannosaurus

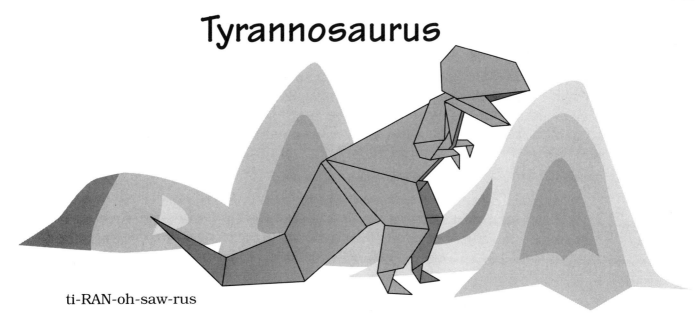

ti-RAN-oh-saw-rus

Probably the largest meat eater ever to walk the earth, this "tyrant lizard" was up to 50 feet long. The 6 inch dagger-like teeth were perfect for eating other Cretaceous animals. Once thought to be feared, some paleontologists now believe it was a scavenger, and could be easily beaten in a fight. Its arms were so small and weak that it probably could not get up if knocked over by the swing of a heavy tail. It used its claws like knives but could not reach its hand to its mouth.

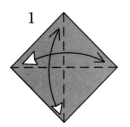

1

Fold and unfold along the diagonals.

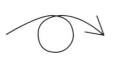

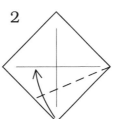

2

Crease lightly.

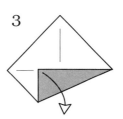

3

Unfold.

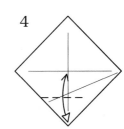

4

Fold up to the center and unfold. Crease lightly and only on the left side.

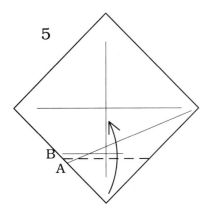

5

Fold up so that A meets the line above it, close to B.

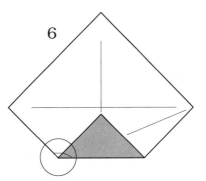

6

Note how the creases intersect inside the circle.

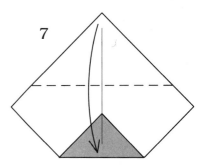

7

8

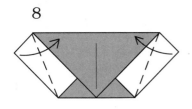

9

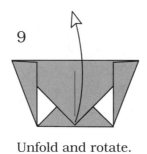

Unfold and rotate.

10

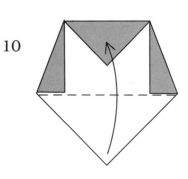

11

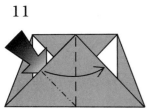

Squash-fold.

12

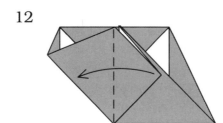

13

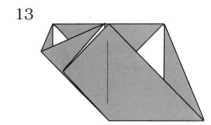

Repeat steps 11–12 on the right.

14

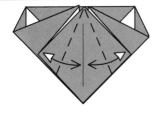

Fold and unfold.

15

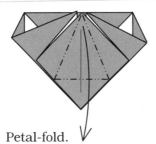

Petal-fold.

16

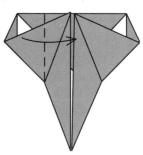

17

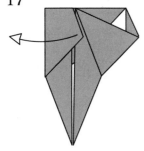

Unfold.

18

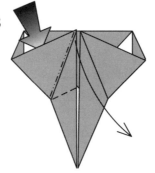

Squash-fold.

19

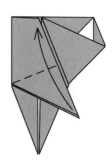

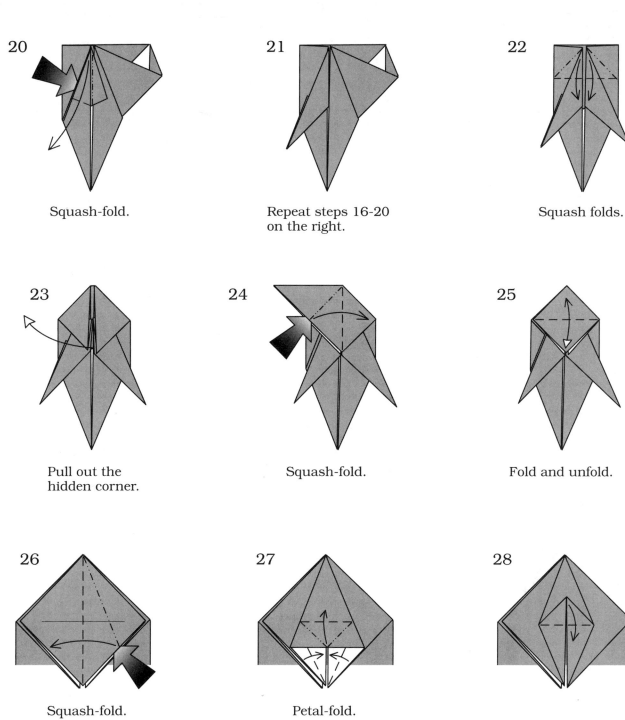

20 Squash-fold.

21 Repeat steps 16-20 on the right.

22 Squash folds.

23 Pull out the hidden corner.

24 Squash-fold.

25 Fold and unfold.

26 Squash-fold.

27 Petal-fold.

28

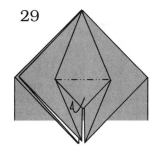

29

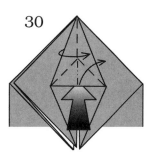

30

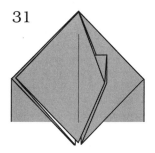

31 Repeat steps 26–30 on the left.

32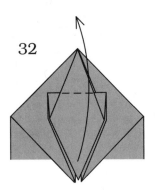

33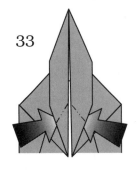

Reverse folds.

34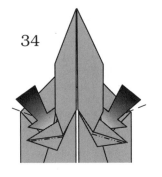

Reverse folds.

35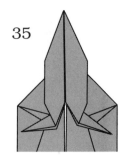

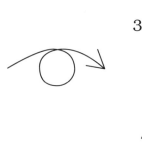

36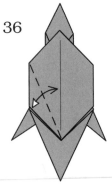

Fold and unfold.

37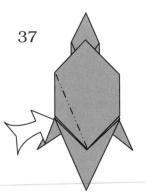

Sink.

38

Do not fold to a point at the top.

39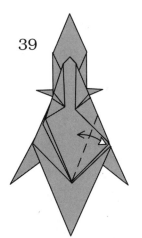

Fold and unfold.

40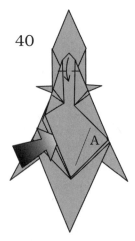

Fold the mouth down. Later, region A will be tucked inside the pocket shown with the arrow.

41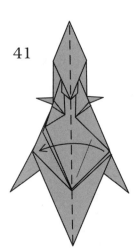

42

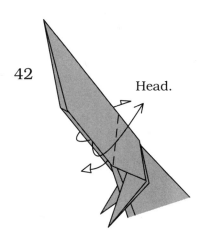

Head.

Outside-reverse-fold and pull out the mouth.

43

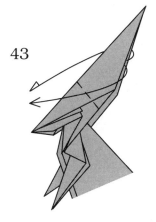

Outside-reverse-fold.

44

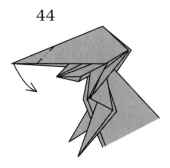

Reverse-fold.

45

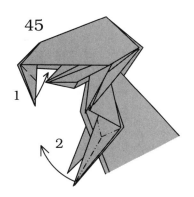

1. A simple valley fold.
2. Double-rabbit-ear, repeat behind.

46

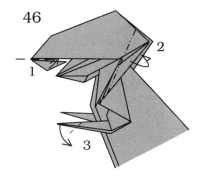

1. Tuck inside.
2. Repeat behind.
3. Reverse-fold, repeat behind.

47

Hind legs and tail.

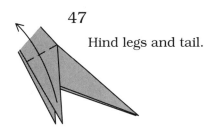

Repeat behind.

48

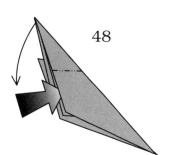

Reverse-fold, repeat behind.

49

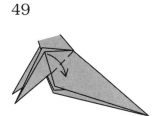

Repeat behind.

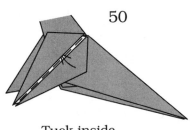

50

Tuck inside,
repeat behind.

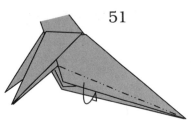

51

Repeat behind.

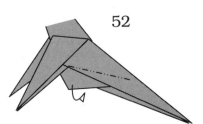

52

Tuck inside the pocket.

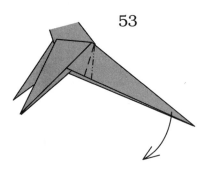

53

Outside-crimp-fold
the tail.

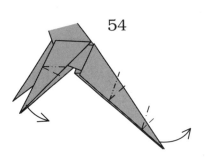

54

Crimp folds, repeat behind.

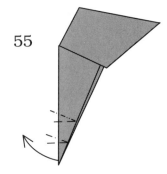

55

Form the feet with crimp
folds, repeat behind.

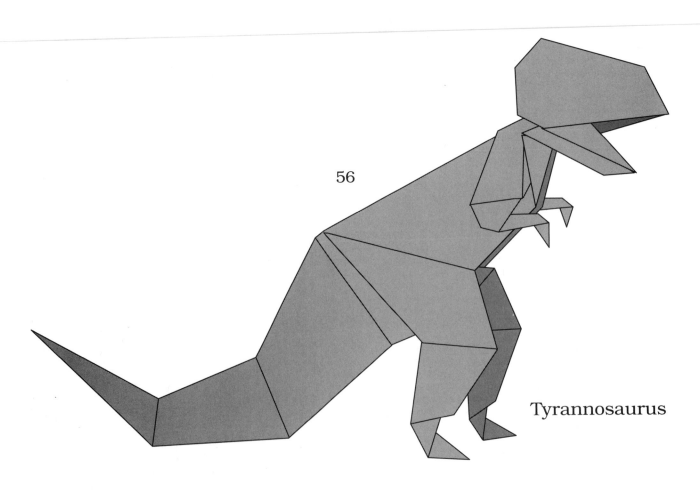

56

Tyrannosaurus

Hadrosaurus

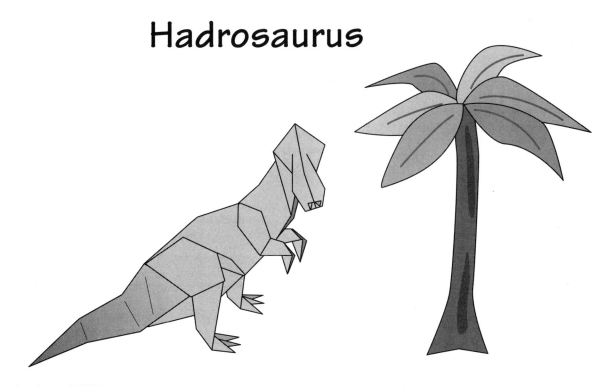

had-ro-SAW-rus

Formerly known as Trachodon, the "rough tooth", this duck billed dinosaur was 33 feet long. Behind the bill were 2000 teeth used for grinding water plants. Hadrosaurus means "bulky lizard" and was the first dinosaur skeleton ever excavated in the U.S. It was found in New Jersey in 1858. Mummified skin has also been found of this Cretaceous creature.

1
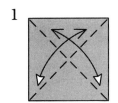
Fold and unfold.

2
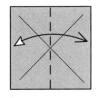
Fold and unfold.

3

4

5
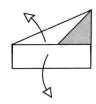
Unfold.

6
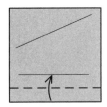

7
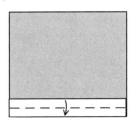

8
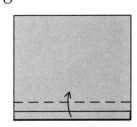
Fold along the existing crease.

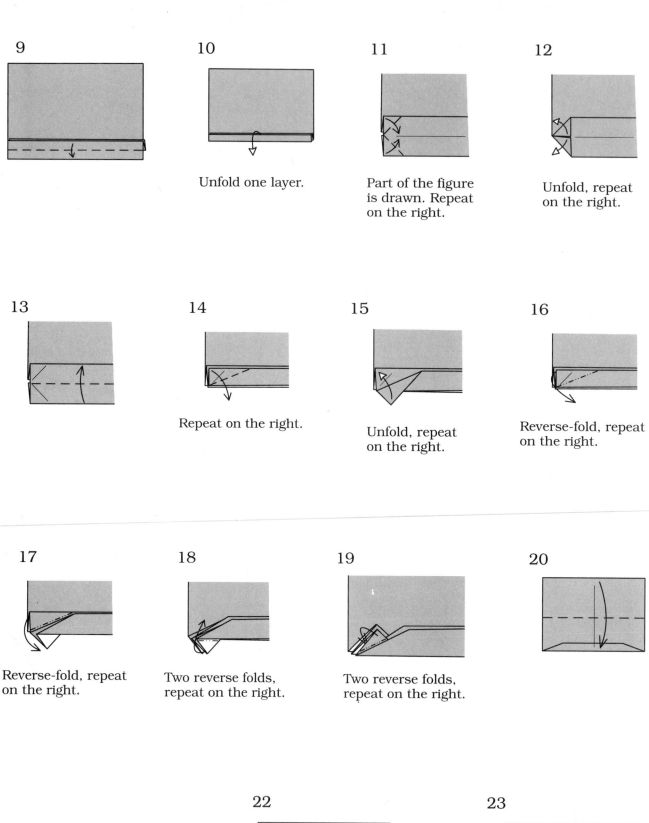

9

10

Unfold one layer.

11

Part of the figure is drawn. Repeat on the right.

12

Unfold, repeat on the right.

13

14

Repeat on the right.

15

Unfold, repeat on the right.

16

Reverse-fold, repeat on the right.

17

Reverse-fold, repeat on the right.

18

Two reverse folds, repeat on the right.

19

Two reverse folds, repeat on the right.

20

21

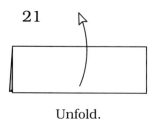

Unfold.

22

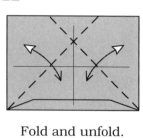

Fold and unfold.

23

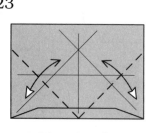

Fold and unfold.

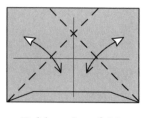

24

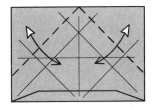

Fold and unfold.

25

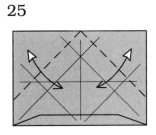

Fold and unfold.

26

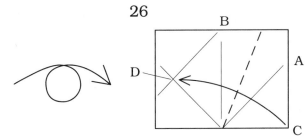

Fold A to B and C to D.

27

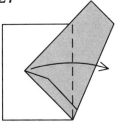

28

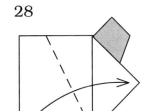

29

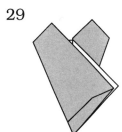

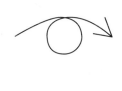

30

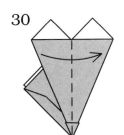

31

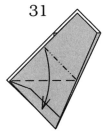

Squash-fold.

32

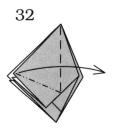

Repeat behind.

33

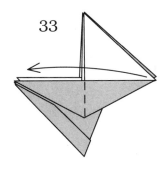

Repeat behind.

34

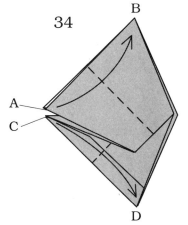

Fold A to B and C to
D, repeat behind.

35

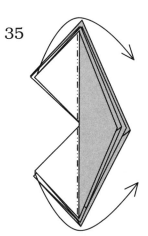

Reverse folds,
repeat behind.

36

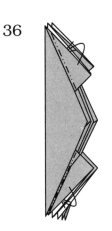

Four reverse folds.

37

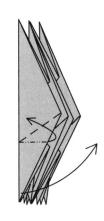

Repeat behind.

Hadrosaurus 87

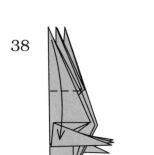

38

39

40

Repeat behind.

Tuck behind.

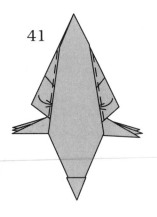

41

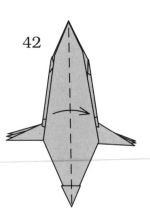

42

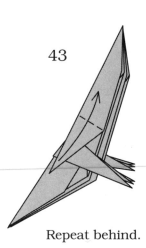

43

Repeat behind.

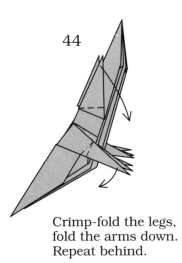

44

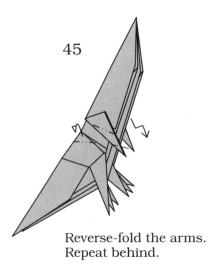

45

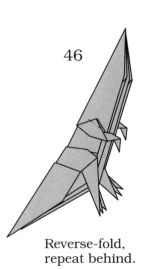

46

Crimp-fold the legs,
fold the arms down.
Repeat behind.

Reverse-fold the arms.
Repeat behind.

Reverse-fold,
repeat behind.

47

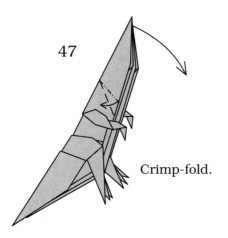

Crimp-fold.

48

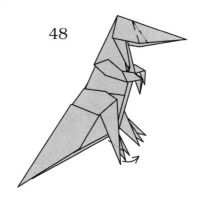

Flatten the head to form a beak. Make reverse folds to form the six toes.

Top view of head.

49

50

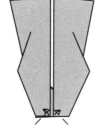

Fold the tip inside.

51

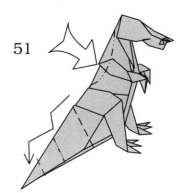

52

Hadrosaurus

Iguanodon

i-GWA-no-don

The most distinguishing feature of this Cretaceous dinosaur is the spike-like thumbs on its front legs. Standing on its hind legs, this reptile stood 16 feet tall. However, it could have also walked on four legs. It had grinding teeth in the back of its mouth and a strong beak with which to break off plants. One of the first dinosaurs ever discovered, fossils were found in Belguim and North Africa. Iguanodon means "iguana tooth".

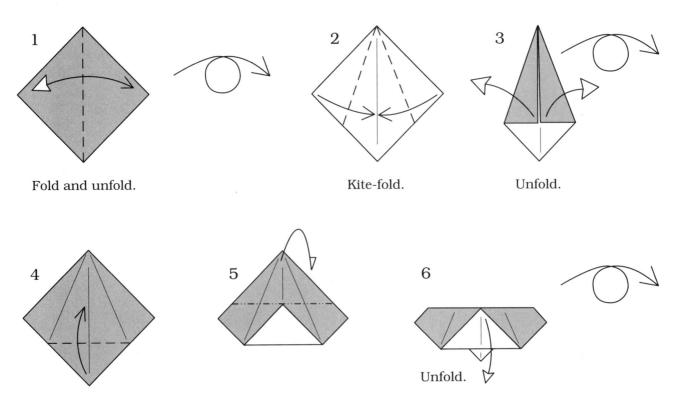

1

Fold and unfold.

2

Kite-fold.

3

Unfold.

4

5

6

Unfold.

7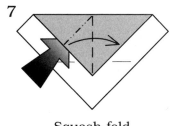

Squash-fold.

8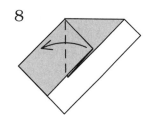

9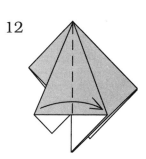

Repeat steps 7–8
on the right.

10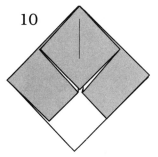

11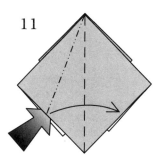

Squash-fold.

12

13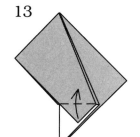

14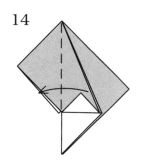

15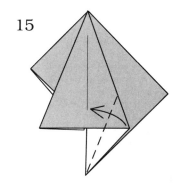

16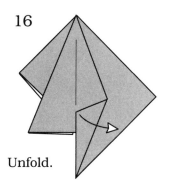

Unfold.

17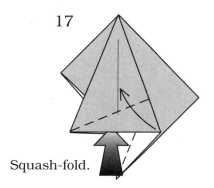

Squash-fold.

18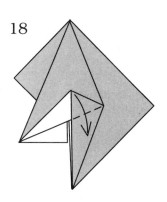

Iguanodon 91

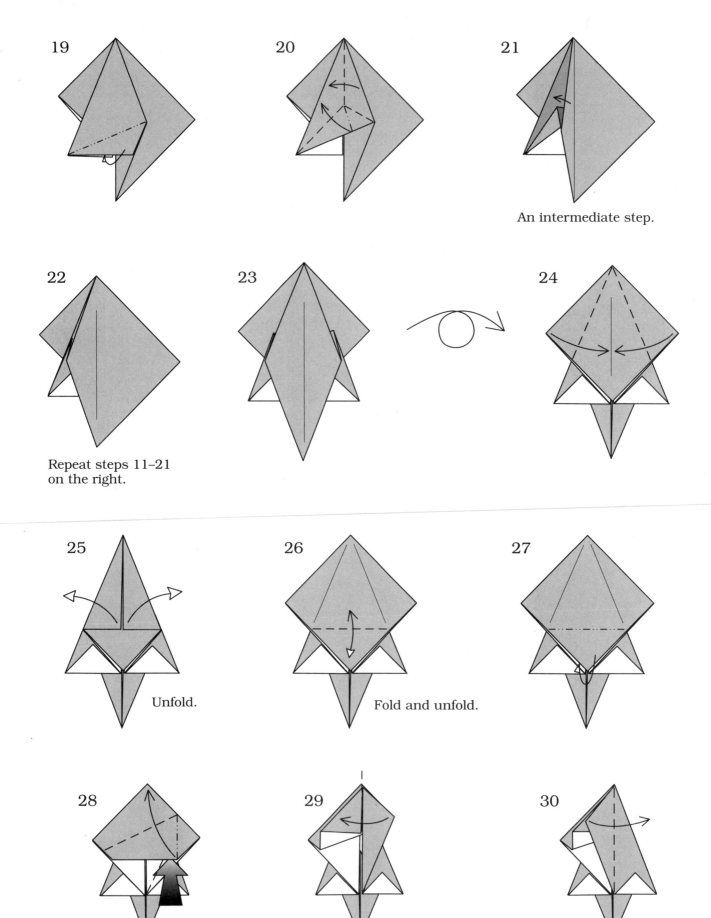

19

20

21

An intermediate step.

22

Repeat steps 11–21
on the right.

23

24

25

Unfold.

26

Fold and unfold.

27

28

Squash-fold.

29

30

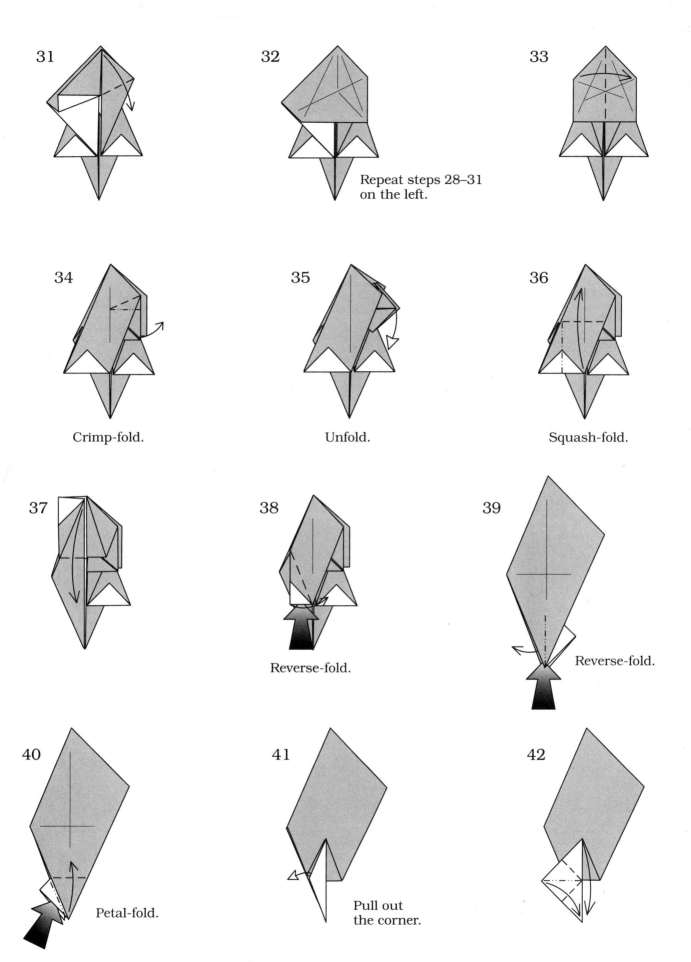

31

32

Repeat steps 28–31
on the left.

33

34

Crimp-fold.

35

Unfold.

36

Squash-fold.

37

38

Reverse-fold.

39

Reverse-fold.

40

Petal-fold.

41

Pull out
the corner.

42

43

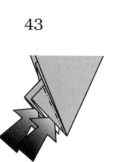

Reverse folds.

44

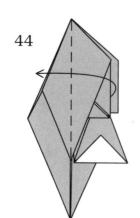

45

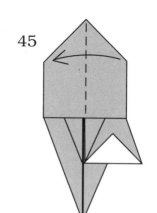

46

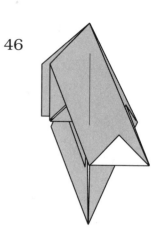

Repeat steps 36–44 on the right.

47

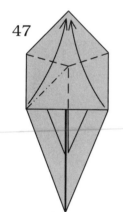

Bring the corners to the top.

48

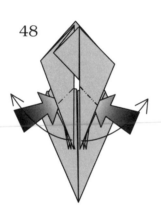

Reverse folds.

49

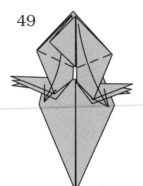

50

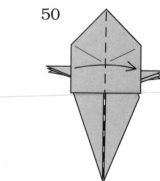

51

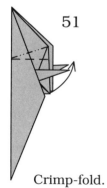

Crimp-fold.

52

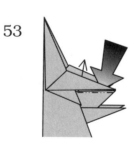

Repeat behind.

53

Reverse-fold.

54

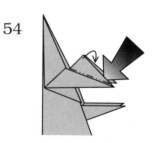

Reverse-fold.

55

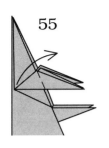

Repeat behind.

56

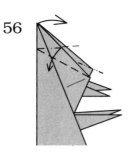

Crimp-fold.

57

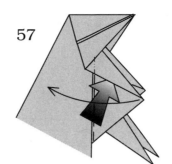

Reverse-fold, repeat behind.

58

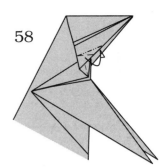

Repeat behind.

59

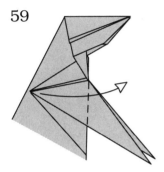

Unfold, repeat behind.

60

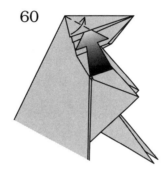

Unlock the top layer, repeat behind.

61

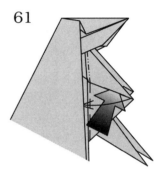

Reverse-fold, tuck under the top layer. Repeat behind.

62

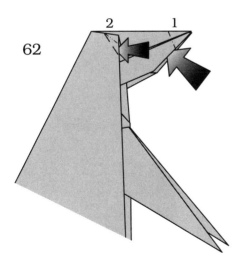

1. Reverse-fold the tip.
2. Squash-fold the eye, repeat behind.

63

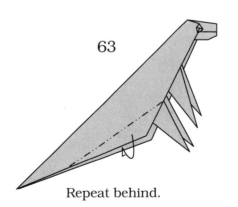

Repeat behind.

64

Legs.

Reverse-fold, repeat behind.

65

Reverse folds, repeat behind.

66

Arms.

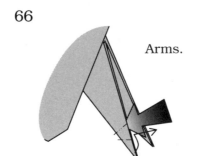

Form the thumb with two reverse folds, repeat behind.

67

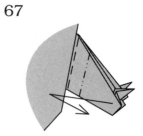

Repeat behind.

68

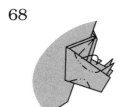

Shape the arms and hands, repeat behind.

69

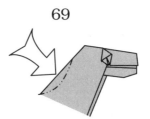

Shape the neck.

70

Tail.

Crimp-fold the tail.

Iguanodon

71

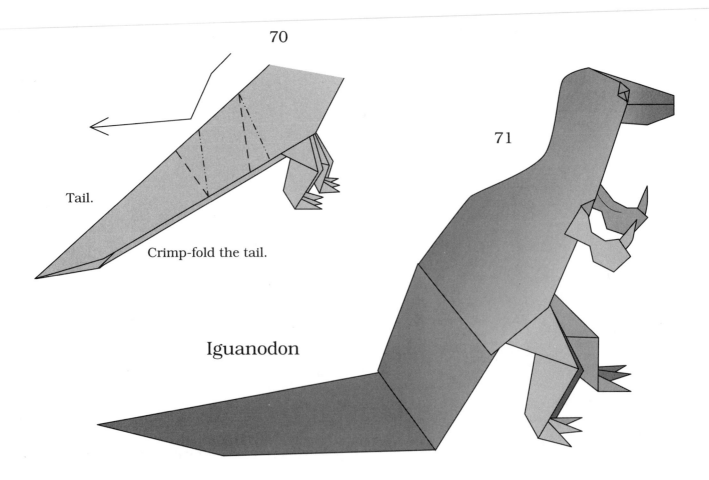

Protoceratops

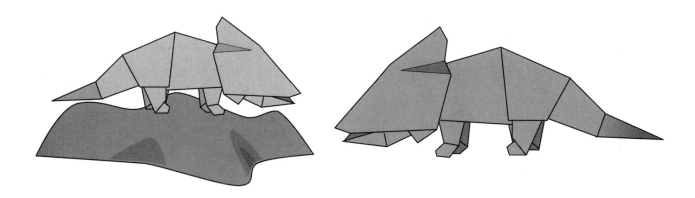

pro-toe-SER-a-tops

The "first horn face" fossils were discovered in Mongolia and showed paleontologists how dinosaurs may have cared for their young. The nests included unhatched eggs as well as skeletons of babies. The adults grew to 6 feet long. These were Cretaceous plant eaters with parrot like beaks and bone covered faces.

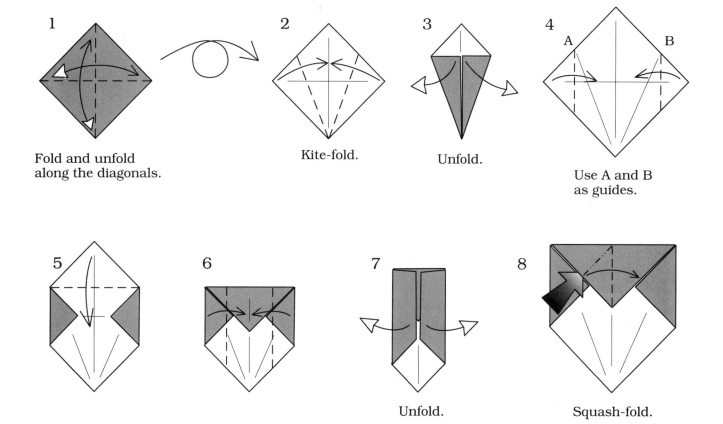

1

Fold and unfold along the diagonals.

2

Kite-fold.

3

Unfold.

4

A   B

Use A and B as guides.

5

6

7

Unfold.

8

Squash-fold.

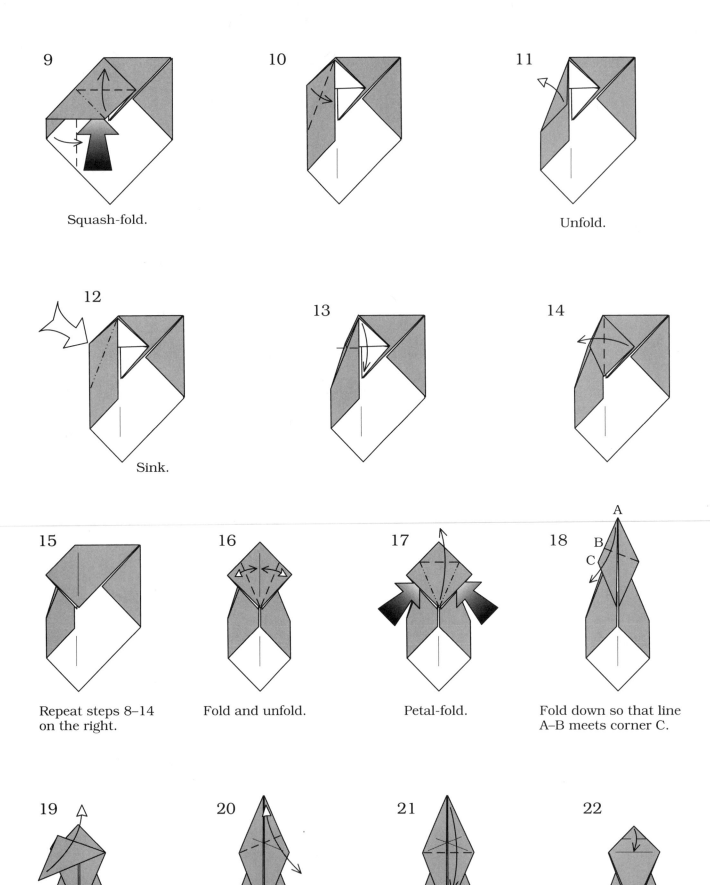

9 Squash-fold.

10

11 Unfold.

12 Sink.

13

14

15 Repeat steps 8–14 on the right.

16 Fold and unfold.

17 Petal-fold.

18 Fold down so that line A–B meets corner C.

A
B
C

19 Unfold.

20 Fold and unfold.

21

22

23

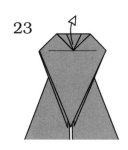

Unfold.

24

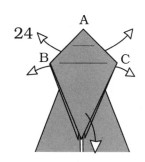

A

B   C

Spread apart and flatten.

25

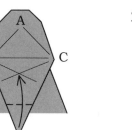

A

B   C

26

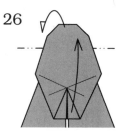

27

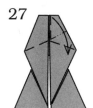

28

29

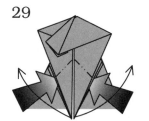

Reverse folds.

30

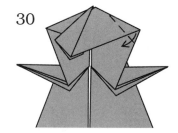

31

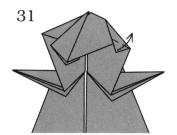

32

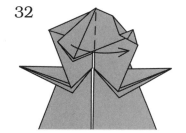

33

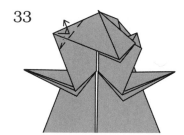

34

35

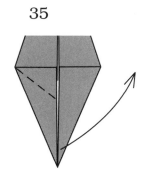

Crease on half of the line.

36

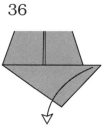

Unfold.

37

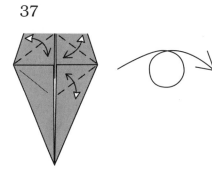

Fold and unfold.

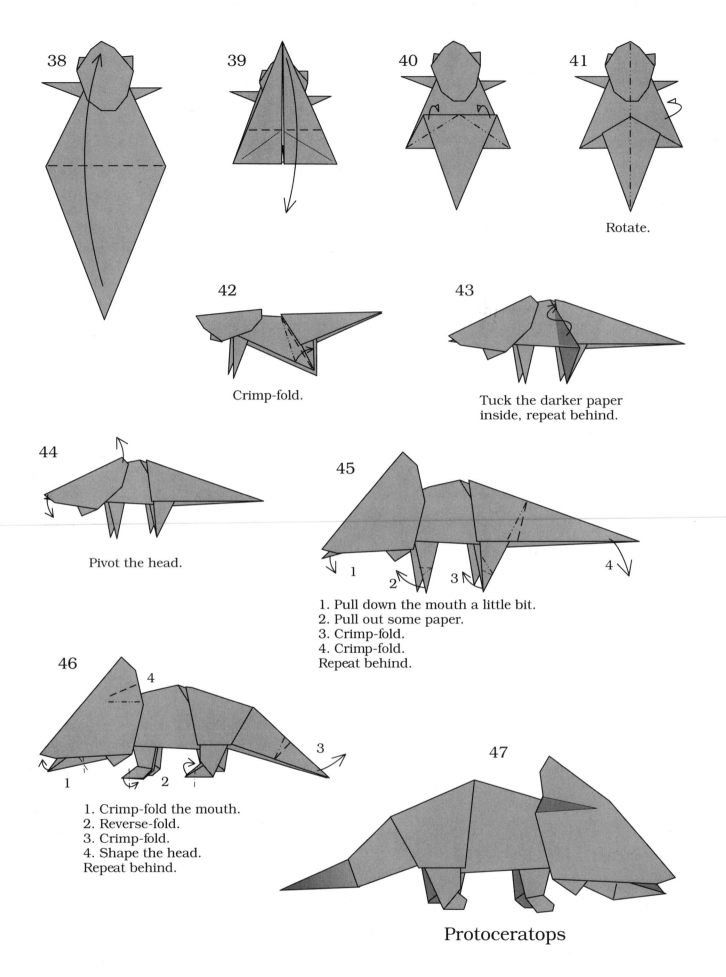

38

39

40

Rotate.

41

42

Crimp-fold.

43

Tuck the darker paper
inside, repeat behind.

44

Pivot the head.

45

1. Pull down the mouth a little bit.
2. Pull out some paper.
3. Crimp-fold.
4. Crimp-fold.
Repeat behind.

46

1. Crimp-fold the mouth.
2. Reverse-fold.
3. Crimp-fold.
4. Shape the head.
Repeat behind.

47

Protoceratops

Triceratops

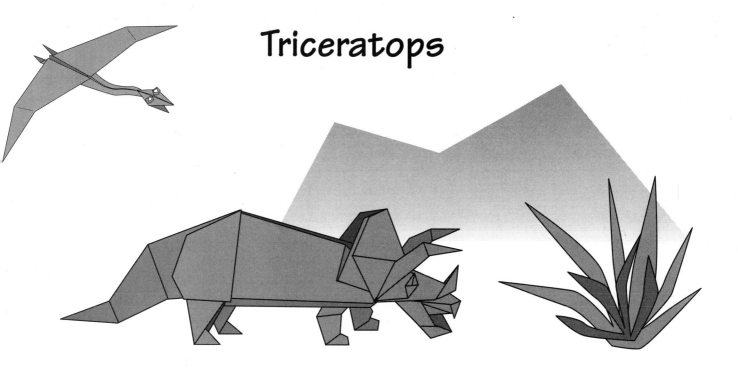

try-SER-a-tops

A peaceful plant eater, Triceratops was 30 feet long. It had a beak like a parrot. Its name means "three horn face" and the horns over its eyes were 3 feet long. The tough, leathery skin and the bony frill protecting its neck made Triceratops one of the best protected dinosaurs. It is thought to be the last one to succumb to extinction at the end of the Cretaceous.

1

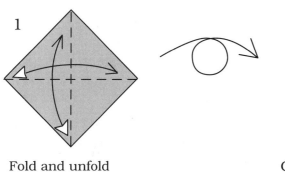

Fold and unfold along the diagonals.

2

Crease lightly as you fold the bottom corner to the center and unfold.

3

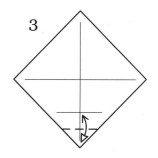

Fold to the crease and unfold.

4

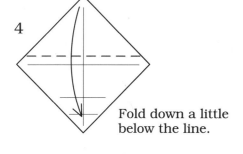

Fold down a little below the line.

5

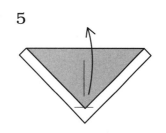

6

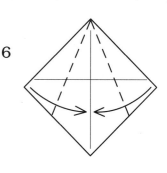

7

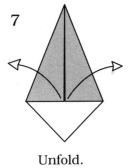

Unfold.

8

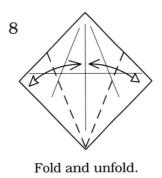

Fold and unfold.

9

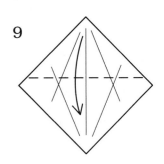

10

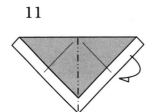

Fold and unfold.

11

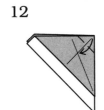

12

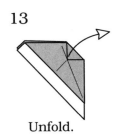

13

Unfold.

14

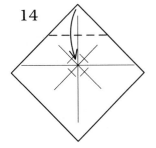

15

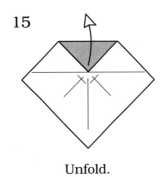

Unfold.

16

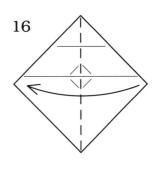

17

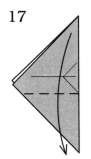

18

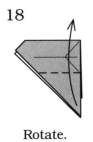

Rotate.

19

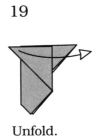

Unfold.

20

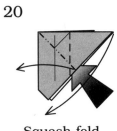

Squash-fold.

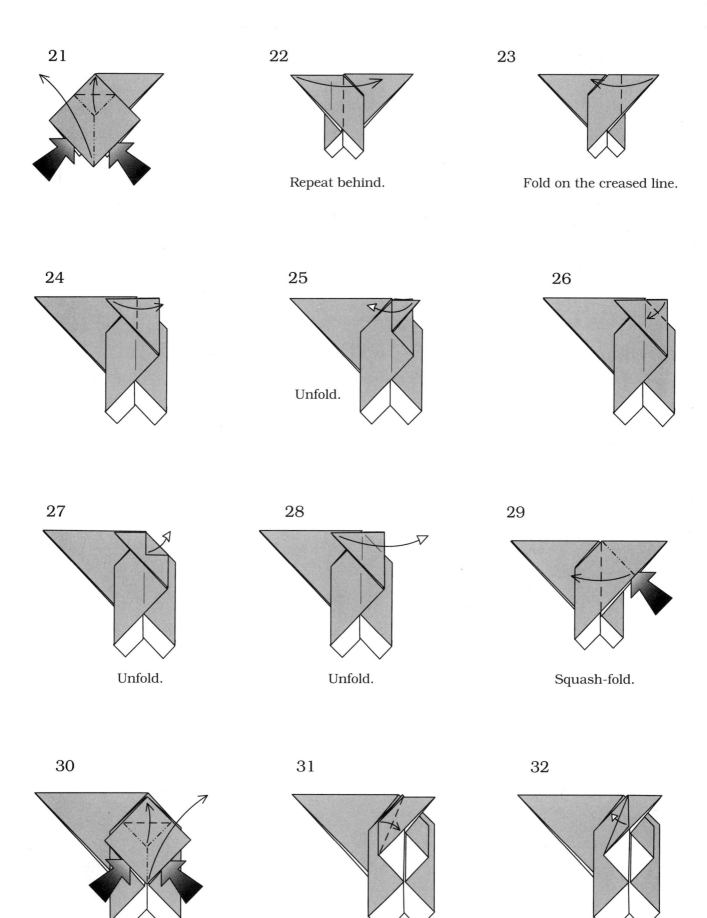

21

22

Repeat behind.

23

Fold on the creased line.

24

25

Unfold.

26

27

Unfold.

28

Unfold.

29

Squash-fold.

30

31

32

Unfold.

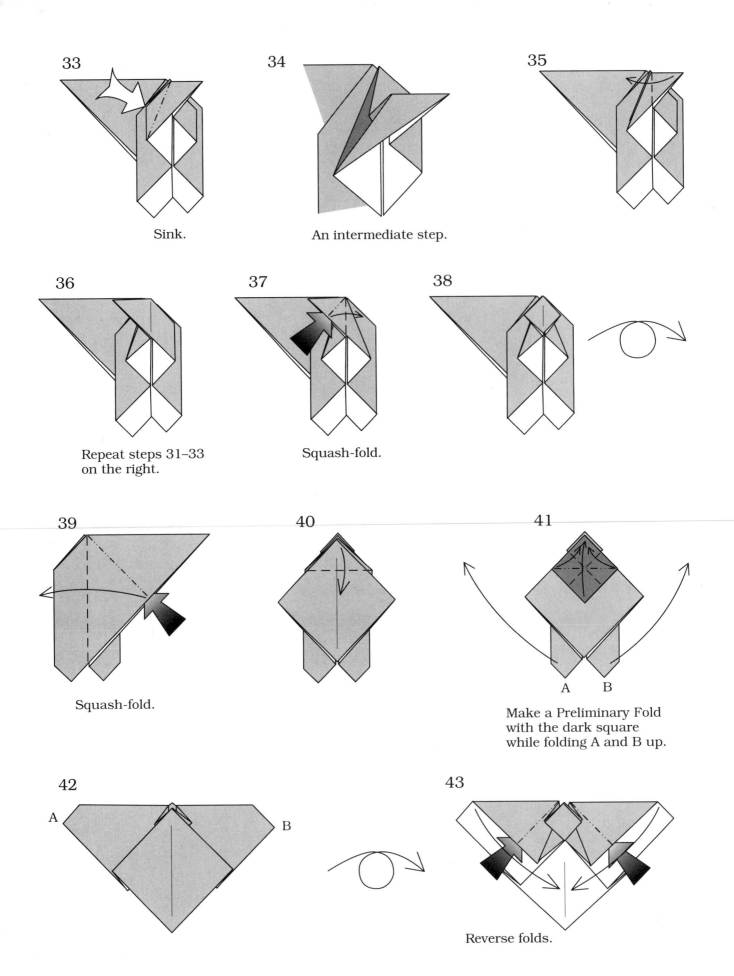

33

Sink.

34

An intermediate step.

35

36

Repeat steps 31–33 on the right.

37

Squash-fold.

38

39

Squash-fold.

40

41

A   B

Make a Preliminary Fold with the dark square while folding A and B up.

42

A   B

43

Reverse folds.

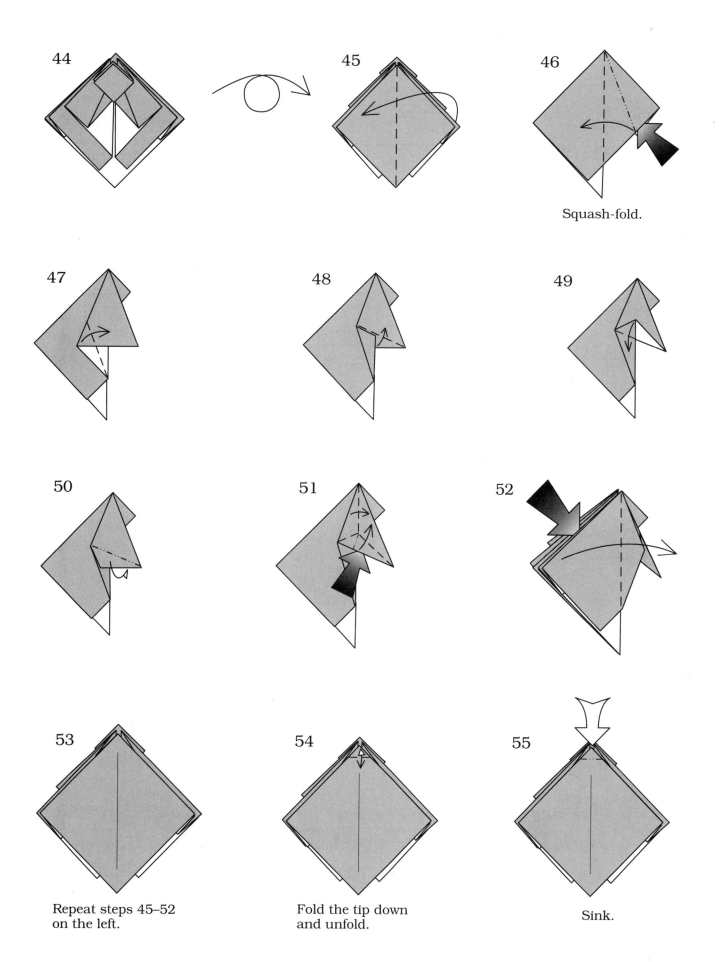

44

45

46

Squash-fold.

47

48

49

50

51

52

53

Repeat steps 45–52
on the left.

54

Fold the tip down
and unfold.

55

Sink.

56

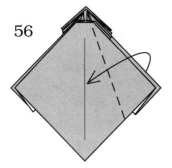

57

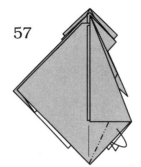

58

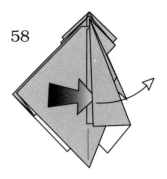

Unfold the top layer.

59

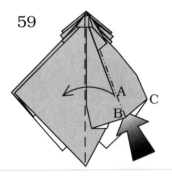

This is a three-dimensional figure.

60

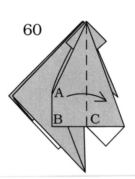

61

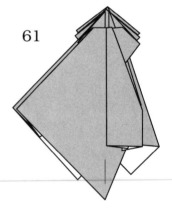

Repeat steps 56–60 on the left.

62

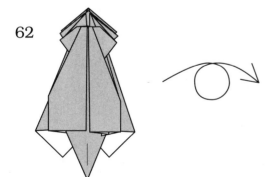

63

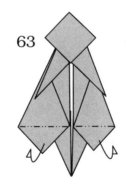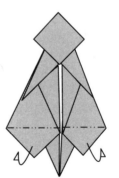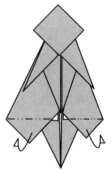

Hopefully your model matches one of these. They are all fine, and differ from the estimated fold in step 4. Be sure that the two mountain folds lie on the same line.

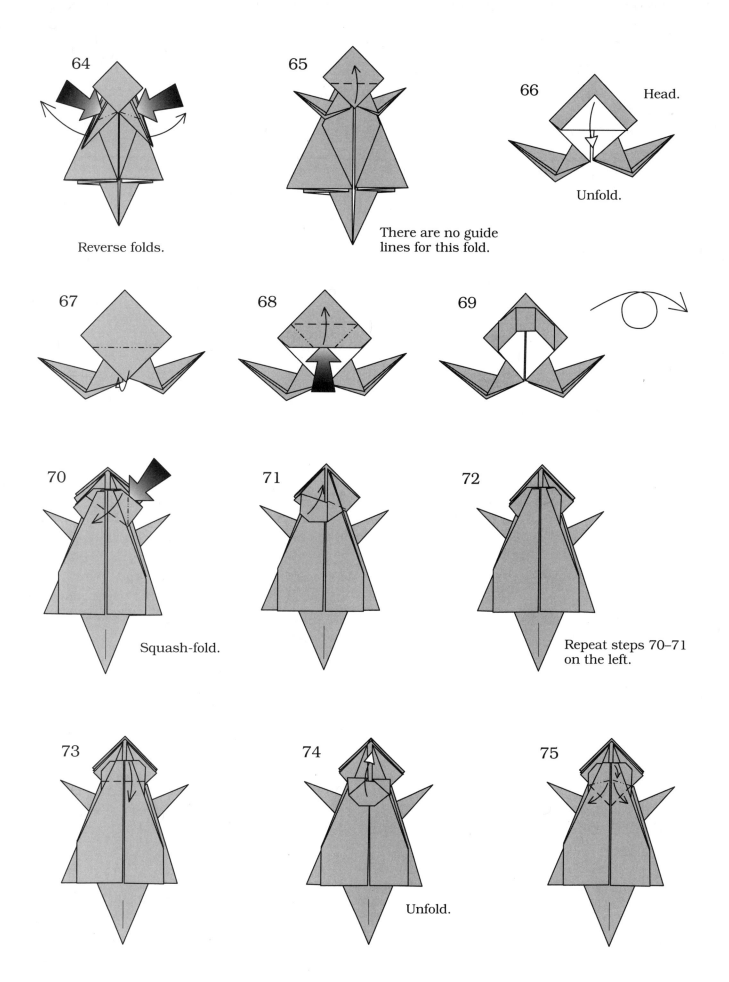

64

Reverse folds.

65

There are no guide lines for this fold.

66 Head.

Unfold.

67

68

69

70

Squash-fold.

71

72

Repeat steps 70–71 on the left.

73

74

Unfold.

75

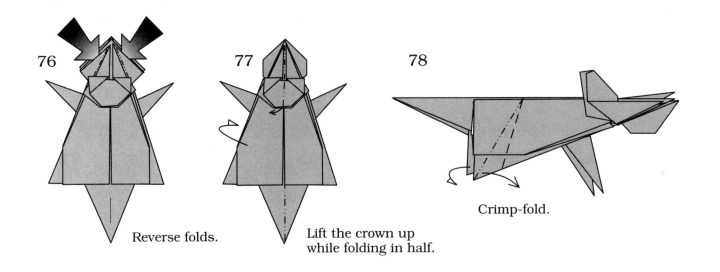

76

Reverse folds.

77

Lift the crown up
while folding in half.

78

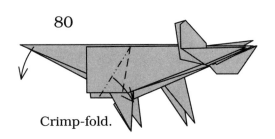

Crimp-fold.

79

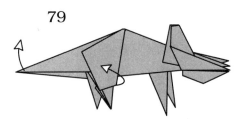

Pull the tail out and unlock the paper
by the hind legs. Repeat behind.

80

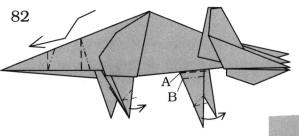

Crimp-fold.

81

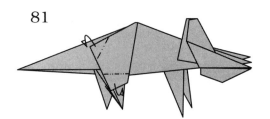

Repeat behind.

82

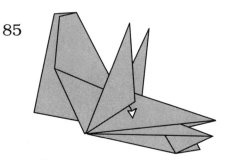

A
B

Repeat behind. Note that lines A and B
are simple folds, not reverse folds. See
the drawing of the finished front leg.

83

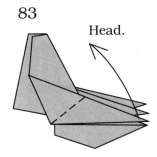

Head.

Repeat behind.

84

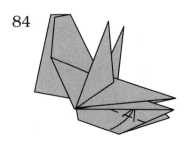

Repeat behind.

85

Pull out, repeat behind.

86

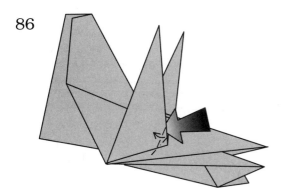

Squash-fold to form
the eye, repeat behind.

87

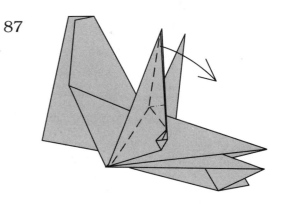

Rabbit-ear, repeat behind.

88

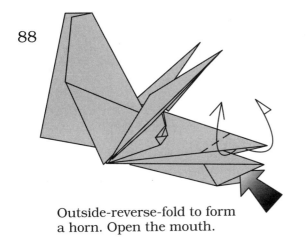

Outside-reverse-fold to form
a horn. Open the mouth.

89

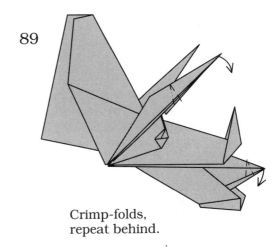

Crimp-folds,
repeat behind.

90

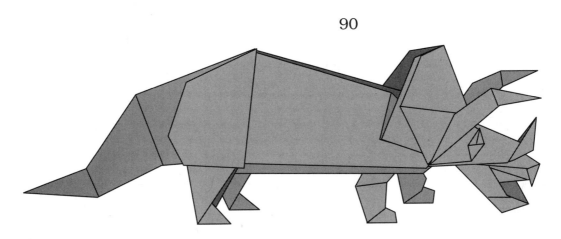

Triceratops

Stegosaurus

steg-oh-SAW-rus

This unique dinosaur was 29 feet long and lived in the Jurassic and early Cretaceous. The plates on its back were to regulate its body heat. It had two walnut size brains. One brain was in its head and the other was at the base of its tail. This "roof lizard" was found in the western U.S. and ate plants.

1

2

3

Fold and unfold.

4

5

6

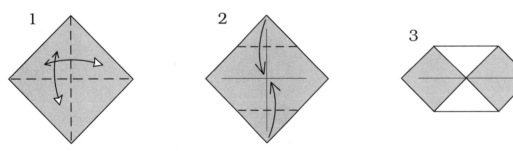

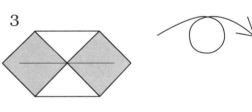

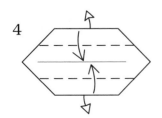

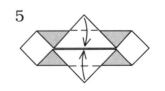

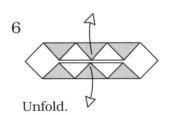

Unfold.

7

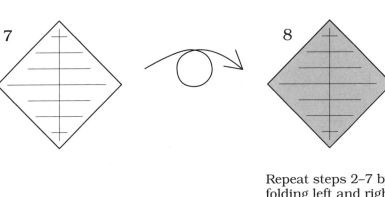

8

Repeat steps 2–7 by folding left and right.

9

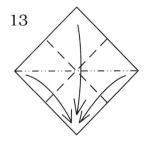

Fold and unfold.

10

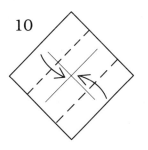

11

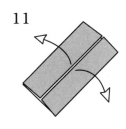

Unfold.

12

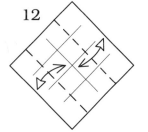

Fold and unfold.

13

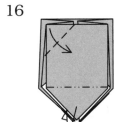

Make the Preliminary Fold.

14

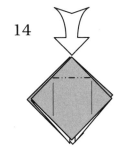

Sink.

15

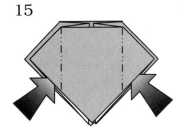

Reverse folds, repeat behind.

16

Repeat behind at the bottom.

17

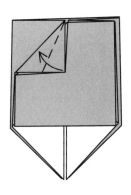

18

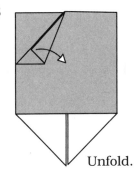

Unfold.

19

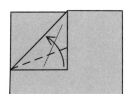

20

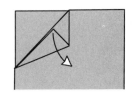

Unfold.

Stegosaurus 111

21

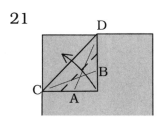

Bring point A and B
up to line C–D.

22

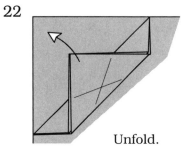

Unfold.

23

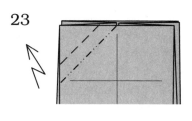

Sink in and out.

24

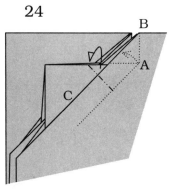

Fold the hidden corner,
A, to line B–C.

25

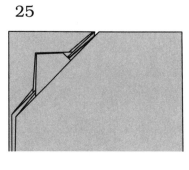

Repeat step 24 three times.

26

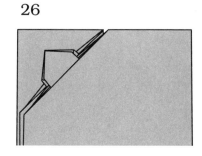

Repeat steps 16 to 25 three
times; on the right and back.

27

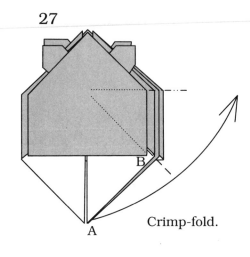

Crimp-fold.

28

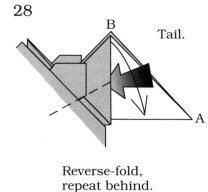

Tail.

Reverse-fold,
repeat behind.

29

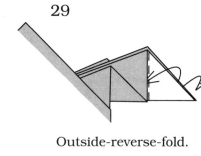

Outside-reverse-fold.

30

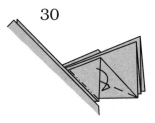

Reverse-fold,
repeat behind.

31

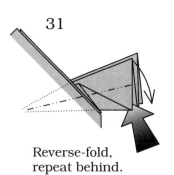

Reverse-fold,
repeat behind.

32

Reverse-fold,
repeat behind.

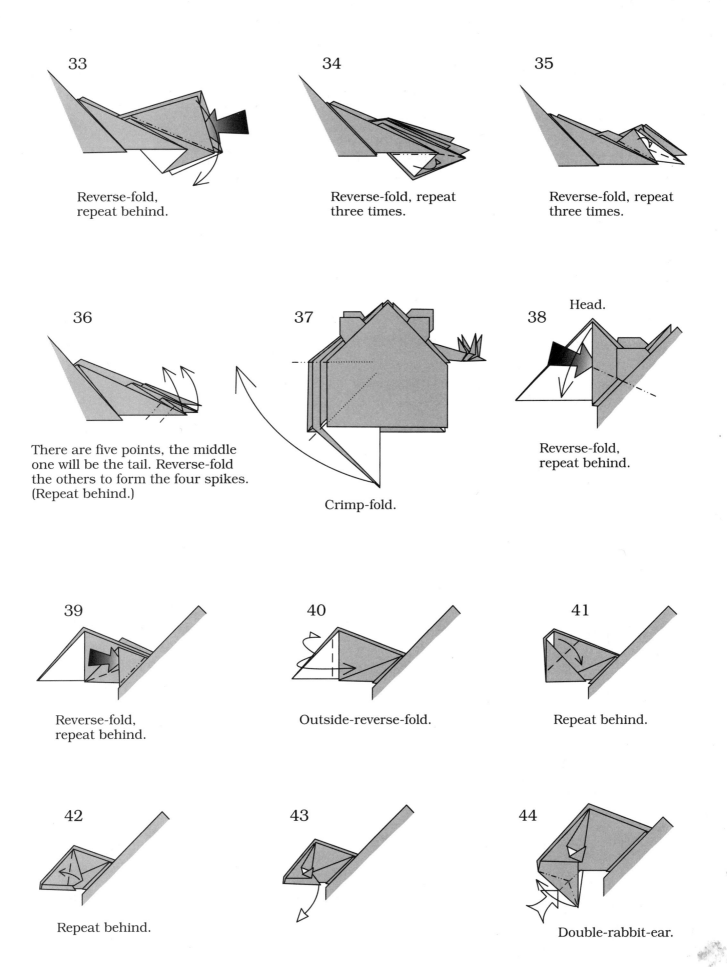

33

Reverse-fold, repeat behind.

34

Reverse-fold, repeat three times.

35

Reverse-fold, repeat three times.

36

There are five points, the middle one will be the tail. Reverse-fold the others to form the four spikes. (Repeat behind.)

37

Crimp-fold.

38

Head.

Reverse-fold, repeat behind.

39

Reverse-fold, repeat behind.

40

Outside-reverse-fold.

41

Repeat behind.

42

Repeat behind.

43

44

Double-rabbit-ear.

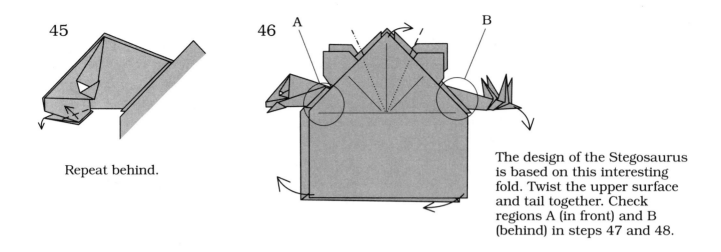

45

Repeat behind.

46

The design of the Stegosaurus is based on this interesting fold. Twist the upper surface and tail together. Check regions A (in front) and B (behind) in steps 47 and 48.

Since the folding is no longer symmetrical, be sure to orient your model according to the drawings.

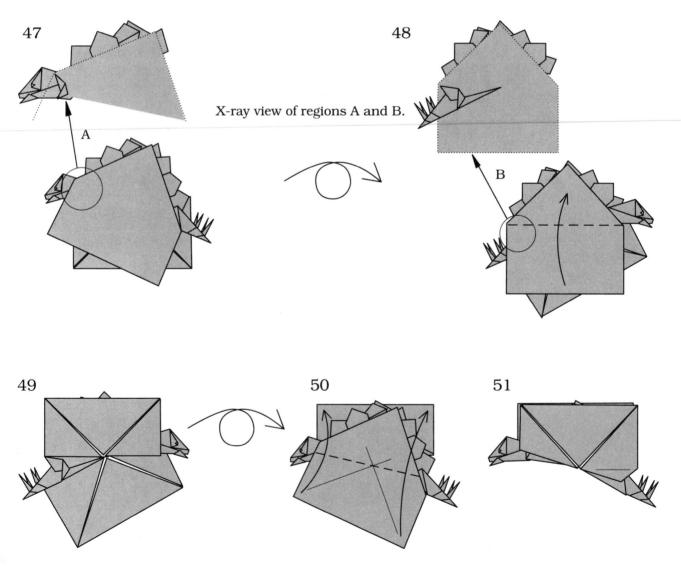

47

A

X-ray view of regions A and B.

48

B

49

50

51

52

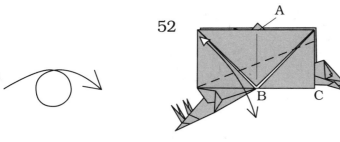

Fold down so that point A lies on line B–C. Unfold.

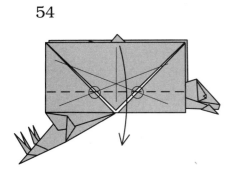

53

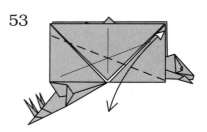

Fold and unfold.

54

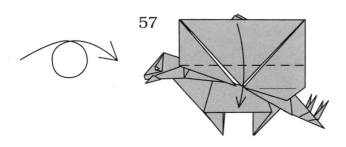

55

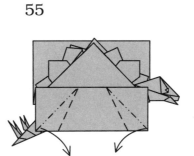

56

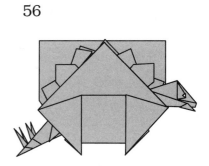

57

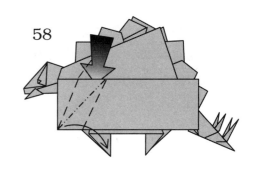

58

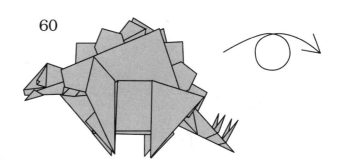

59

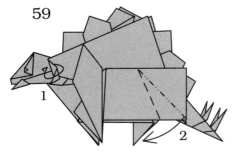

1. Fold inside-out to form a plate near the head.
2. Form a leg.

60

Stegosaurus 115

61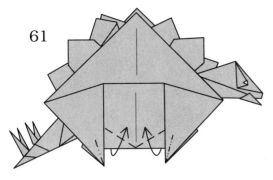

Repeat behind.

62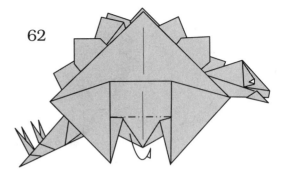

Repeat behind.

63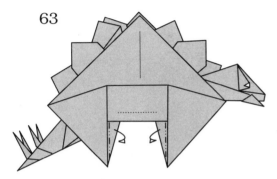

Mountain-fold on the
x-ray line, repeat behind.

64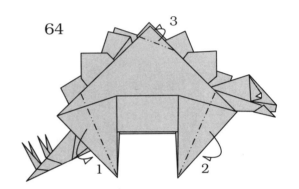

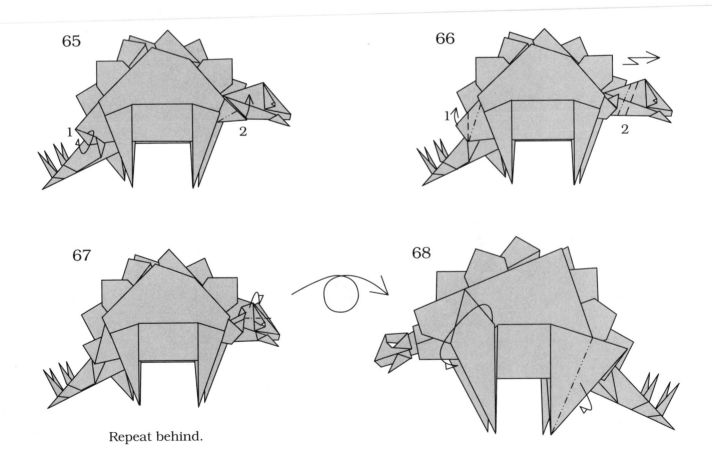

Repeat behind.

69
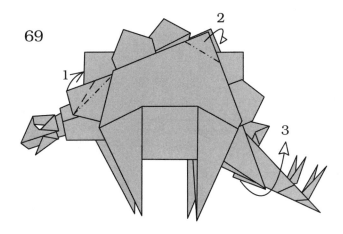

70

Repeat behind.

71

Stegosaurus

Basic Folds

Rabbit Ear.

To fold a rabbit ear, one corner is folded in half and laid down to a side.

1
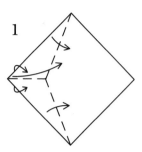

Fold a rabbit ear.

2
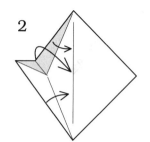

A three-dimensional intermediate step.

3
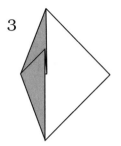

Double Rabbit Ear.

If you were to bend a straw you would be folding the double rabbit ear.

1
2
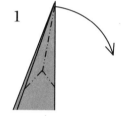

(Straw)

1
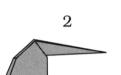

Make a double rabbit ear.

2
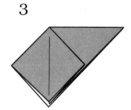

Squash Fold.

In a squash fold, some paper is opened and then made flat. The shaded arrow shows where to place your finger.

1
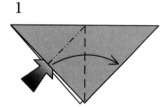

Squash-fold.

2
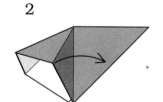

A three-dimensional intermediate step.

3
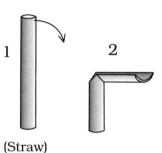

Petal Fold.

In a petal fold, one point is folded up while two opposite sides meet each other.

1
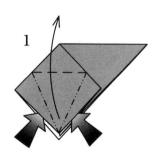

Petal-fold.

2
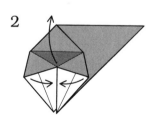

A three-dimensional intermediate step.

3
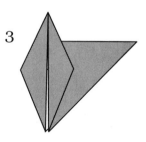

Inside Reverse Fold.

In an inside reverse fold, some paper is folded between layers. Here are two examples.

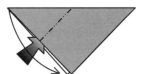

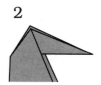

Reverse-fold.

Reverse-fold.

Outside Reverse Fold.

Much of the paper must be unfolded to make an outside reverse fold.

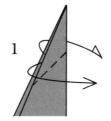

Outside-reverse-fold.

Crimp Fold.

A crimp fold is a combination of two reverse folds.

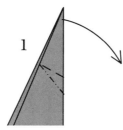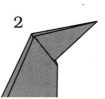

Crimp-fold.

Sink Fold.

In a sink fold, some of the paper without edges is folded inside. To do this fold, much of the model must be unfolded.

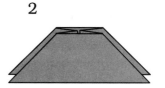

Sink.

Spread Squash Fold.

A cross between a squash fold and sink fold, some paper in the center is spread apart and then made flat.

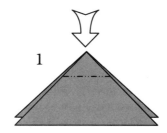

Spread-squash-fold.